102 029 748 4

Busi
Strat

for volu

Alan Lawrie

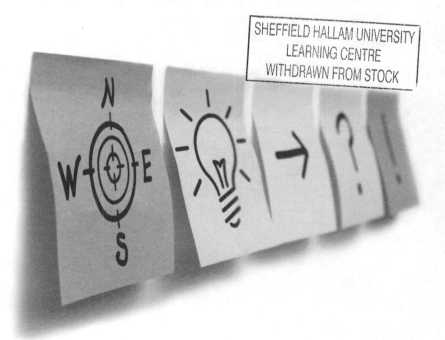

DIRECTORY OF SOCIAL CHANGE

Fourth edition

Published by the Directory of Social Change (Registered Charity no. 800517 in England and Wales)
Head office: 24 Stephenson Way, London NW1 2DP
Northern office: Suite 103, 1 Old Hall Street, Liverpool L3 9HG
Tel: 08450 77 77 07

Visit www.dsc.org.uk to find out more about our books, subscription funding websites and training events. You can also sign up for e-newsletters so that you're always the first to hear about what's new.

The publisher welcomes suggestions and comments that will help to inform and improve future versions of this and all of our titles. Please give us your feedback by emailing publications@dsc.org.uk.

It should be understood that this publication is intended for guidance only and is not a substitute for professional or legal advice. No responsibility for loss occasioned as a result of any person acting or refraining from acting can be accepted by the authors or publisher.

First published 1988
Second edition 1994
Reprinted revised second edition 2001
Reprinted 2004
Third edition 2007
Fourth edition 2014

ISBN 978 1 906294 84 7

British Library Cataloguing in Publication Data
A catalogue record for this book is available from the British Library

Cover and text design by Kate Bass
Typeset by Marlinzo Services, Frome
Printed and bound by Page Bros, Norwich

MIX
Paper from
responsible sources
FSC
www.fsc.org
FSC® C023114

Contents

Chapter seven

Developing options and setting the strategic direction   105

Chapter eight

Resourcing the plan   137

Chapter nine

Establishing credibility   175

Chapter ten
Putting the plan on paper

Chapter eleven
Making it happen

References

Index

About the author

Alan Lawrie has worked as a full-time independent consultant for 20 years and specialises in strategy, business planning, and commissioning and organisational development.

Before moving into consultancy Alan worked as a development worker, trainer and manager in the voluntary sector and then moved into management roles in the public sector.

He is the author of *Managing Quality of Service* (1984 and 1995), *Developing Your Organisation* (2000), *The Complete Guide to Business and Strategic Planning* (1988, 1994 and 2007), *Managing Contracts: A Resources Pack* (1988 and 1994), *The Complete Guide to Creating and Managing New Projects* (1999, 2002 and 2010) and co-author of *The Complete Guide to Surviving Contracts* (2008) and *Collaborative Working* (2013).

Alan has helped many organisations to develop strategies and worked with them to create successful business plans.

Acknowledgements

The author and publisher are grateful to Kogan Page for permission to use and adapt ideas from *The Strategic Planning* Workbook by Neville Lake, to John Wiley & Sons, Inc. for permission to reproduce and adapt the Business Model Canvas by Osterwalder and Pigneur, and to McKinsey & Company for permission to reproduce the 7-S framework.

About the Directory of Social Change

The Directory of Social Change (DSC) has a vision of an independent voluntary sector at the heart of social change. The activities of independent charities, voluntary organisations and community groups are fundamental to achieve social change. We exist to help these organisations and the people who support them to achieve their goals.

We do this by:

- providing practical tools that organisations and activists need, including online and printed publications, training courses, and conferences on a huge range of topics;
- acting as a 'concerned citizen' in public policy debates, often on behalf of smaller charities, voluntary organisations and community groups;
- leading campaigns and stimulating debate on key policy issues that affect those groups;
- carrying out research and providing information to influence policymakers.

DSC is the leading provider of information and training for the voluntary sector and publishes an extensive range of guides and handbooks covering subjects such as fundraising, management, communication, finance and law. We have a range of subscription-based websites containing a wealth of information on funding from trusts, companies and government sources. We run more than 300 training courses each year, including bespoke in-house training provided at the client's location. DSC conferences, many of which run on an annual basis, include the Charity Management Conference, the Charity Accountants' Conference and the Charity Law Conference. DSC's major annual event is Charityfair, which provides low-cost training on a wide variety of subjects.

For details of all our activities, and to order publications and book courses, go to www.dsc.org.uk, call 08450 777707 or email publications@dsc.org.uk.

Foreword

'Would you tell me, please, which way I ought to go from here?'

'That depends a good deal on where you want to get to,' said the Cat.

'I don't much care where—' said Alice.

'Then it doesn't much matter which way you go,' said the Cat.

'—so long as I get *somewhere*,' Alice added as an explanation.

'Oh, you're sure to do that,' said the Cat, 'if only you walk long enough.'

Lewis Carroll, Alice in Wonderland

- What are you trying to achieve?
- Where will your charity be in five or ten years' time?
- How are you going to get there?
- What difference do you make?

These are four questions that I find myself being asked on a regular basis by our beneficiaries, by our supporters, by key stakeholders and by the media. If you don't have answers to these questions in today's charity landscape, you'll meet barriers and problems.

Of course the voluntary sector has done quite a few spectacular things without having a proper strategic plan. I doubt the Anti-Slavery society spent ages working out their business model, or that the founders of Samaritans, Crisis, ChildLine or Oxfam started off with a detailed five-year plan. They just saw a social need and set about doing something about it. But sooner or later, there comes a point where you have to articulate your vision, and how you're going to go about achieving it. Sometimes it's because funders want to know how their money is going to be spent, sometimes it's because people inside the organisation aren't quite clear what they're there for, and other times it's just because your charity has reached that moment where it needs to decide what it doesn't do, as well as what it does.

Having reached that moment, the prospect of setting a strategy can be terrifying. Who do you ask? Who decides? What's the structure? Where do you start? Some organisations spend a fortune creating their strategy only to discover that they'd forgotten something crucial, or their plans were turned upside down by an event outside their control. We have a strategy at Mind (which is available on our website); it's quite ambitious but well thought through, and wholly informed by the views of people with mental health problems. So far it's going quite well. We won't achieve everything (and we've over-achieved on some others!) but it lets all our stakeholders know what we're planning and how we can help.

So here's a really easy-to-read and easy-to-understand (and inexpensive!) book that will help you create a great strategy and plan. It's friendly and informative. It gives you the right ideas and structures. It can't stop unforeseen events, but it helps you plan for them. By the time you've finished, people in your organisation should be able to answer those four questions and know they're going somewhere.

Paul Farmer, Chief Executive of Mind (www.mind.org.uk)

Chapter one
Introduction

> If you don't know where you are going, you are sure to end up somewhere else.
>
> Lawrence J. Peter, Yogi Berra and others

Developing a strategy and a business plan for a voluntary organisation should be a creative and dynamic process – an opportunity to stand back, review progress and generate a new sense of purpose and direction. It should ensure that the organisation is strong, clear about its priorities and able to make a convincing case for support. However, all too often planning is seen as a chore that takes people away from providing a service, and any plan that is produced is a collection of targets, budgets and intentions that have little grounding in reality.

What this book is about

This book's starting point is that business and strategic planning is an essential and useful process for any organisation. Its main theme is that those who are charged with managing a voluntary organisation must ensure that they set the direction, agree strategies for where they want to go, clarify their long- and short-term goals and make a case for why others should have confidence in their organisation.

In addition to strategic thinking, the book focuses on the process of putting the plan together and turning the ideas and strategies in the plan into action. Business planning is about much more than producing a neat and tidy document. Generating paper plans is easy compared with the hard work of managing change and making plans work in action. Furthermore, the book is concerned with not only producing a credible plan, but also ensuring that the plan feels real and relevant to people in the organisation. Whether it is called a business plan, a strategic plan or a forward plan is not important.

In a nutshell, the book:

1. aims to help voluntary organisations make clear decisions about their future direction and priorities;
2. introduces some tools for strategic planning and management;
3. explains how to draw up and use a business plan.

Some terminology

Different writers, and indeed different funders, use the language of strategic and business planning in various ways. Nevertheless, there are some generally agreed definitions out in the world and they will be defined here in a similar way to show how they are used in this book. In addition, there are many terms to describe the sector and those who benefit (or the positive impact created) as a result of organisations' work. The words chosen and the rationale behind these choices are explained briefly here also. The main point to remember about terminology is that the results matter rather than the names used.

Voluntary or not-for-profit?

With many voluntary organisations run largely or even entirely by paid staff, the term 'voluntary' may seem to be a misnomer and so an alternative term 'not-for-profit' is often used instead. However, it seems odd to describe an organisation by what it doesn't aim to do rather than what it is for. With this in mind, and the fact that there is no term which describes the sector perfectly, this book sticks with the term 'voluntary sector'.

Service user

This term has been used throughout the book for consistency purposes, but can be used interchangeably with 'beneficiary' or 'customer', or whichever word or phrase applies best in your organisation.

Vision, mission and objectives

- **Vision:** a clear, inspirational and memorable statement about what the world will look like if your organisation achieves its aspirations. For example: 'A clean sustainable world for our children'.
- **Mission:** a brief statement of long-term overall intent and purpose: what the organisation is doing to achieve its vision. It is what sets your organisation apart from others. For example, two organisations could have the same vision 'A clean sustainable world for our children' but quite different missions. One may focus on conservation 'to conserve our natural resources on which all life depends' and another on campaigning 'to campaign for action and effective changes in legislation to reverse global warming'.
- **Strategic aims:** a number of quantifiable activities to be completed which will help to achieve the mission and ultimately the vision. They are statements of the key priorities for the organisation in the immediate to medium-term future. Everything the organisation does should be related to a strategic aim.
- **Operational objectives:** these are detailed, costed and timed plans of what the organisation will do under each strategic aim. They set out a work plan for the organisation.
- **Values:** the shared beliefs within the organisation which create its culture and guide how people behave and make decisions.

Chapter 5 expands on these definitions and gives some advice on creating a vision, mission and values.

Outcomes and outputs

- **Outputs** are what the organisation produces or delivers, such as 500 rights guides produced or 44 people trained.
- **Outcomes** are the difference that you make. Some outcomes are about creating a change; others are about preventing something negative from happening. There are short-term outcomes, such as 'people know their rights' and 'jobs created'. These can then lead to an organisation's long-term outcomes, i.e. the vision: 'a world without discrimination' and 'all people with equal opportunities'.

Chapter 5 explores outcomes in relation to inputs and gives advice on how to measure them (see page 55).

Strategic thinking, business planning and strategic management

Strategic thinking and planning are about...	Business planning is about...	Strategic management is about...
<ul><li>how the organisation can best meet its vision;</li><li>learning and involve evaluating current activities, analysing the issues that your organisation is facing and identifying external trends and developments;</li><li>developing ideas about how the organisation should develop, what its priorities are and what roles it should play in the future;</li><li>goals and outcomes: what do you want to change, create or prevent?;</li><li>getting focused and making sure that your goals are clear.</li></ul>	<ul><li>putting the analysis and agreed direction into a formal planning format that can be used to guide the organisation;</li><li>allocating resources to strategic priorities;</li><li>showing/persuading others that the organisation has (or can get) the resources to deliver the strategy: that the plan is credible, achievable and worth backing;</li><li>how the organisation will manage and use its resources to achieve the strategy;</li><li>setting out the outputs that need to be delivered to create the desired outcomes;</li><li>showing that the organisation has the capacity, resources and management ability to achieve the strategy.</li></ul>	<ul><li>the process of creating the strategy and making it happen: ensuring that the business plan is implemented;</li><li>monitoring progress and managing change.</li></ul>

Why bother making a strategy?

You cannot stand still and survive in a rapidly changing world

If an organisation is uncertain about funding, lacks a clear direction, relies on what was done in the past as the basis for deciding what to do next and has a vision that stops at the end of the current financial year, it can easily become motionless. It spends its time hoping that things will get better. In effect, it becomes governed by what it did in the past rather than what it wants to do in the future. It becomes predictable and paralysed in a rapidly changing world.

Nevertheless, however static an organisation becomes, it will naturally arrive at a point where decisions have to be made about its future. A director of one charity described her role as akin to 'riding a rollercoaster that never arrives anywhere, but only gets faster'. Changes in legislation, new funding, short-term priorities and new ways of working mean that organisations react to external events and become pulled into activities that either do not fit with the rest of the organisation or are a departure from their original aims.

Rather than being a hostage to the past or to outside forces, those charged with the management and direction of the organisation need to take a grip on what they are doing. They must be bold enough to suggest a direction to go in and to agree a plan for achieving it, not only respond to external events. They must clarify the aims of their organisation to decide what is and is not a priority, especially given voluntary organisations' limited resources, and to set out a direction for the organisation's future.

This kind of management is different from dealing with the day-to-day demands of making sure that the organisation continues to operate. Indeed, part of thinking strategically is to keep in touch with day-to-day realities and opportunities, but at the same time you need to focus on future needs and directions.

Emergent strategy and deliberate strategy

With this balance between developing emerging opportunities and setting a future direction in mind, an interesting idea to consider is the distinction between emergent strategy and deliberate strategy, as made by the management writer Henry Mintzberg. He outlines how a strategy may be fulfilled without it being intended at all or because other intended strategies were lost over time (Mintzberg 1978). In this way, all organisations are moving in some direction even if they do not know it or have not actively planned it: they respond to events, experiment and follow up opportunities and this forms a direction.

What organisations do is usually determined by a mixture of deliberate strategy (formal plans, budgets and written work programmes) and emergent strategy. Deliberate strategists like things to be under control, be structured and follow a clear pattern. Emergent strategists are prepared to let things happen, respond to opportunities and resist attempts to control or over-programme activities.

So, although we cannot always control the detail, an organisation is going to keep moving and changing anyway, and so it is better to chart its path than let it happen by accident. Both deliberate and emergent strategies have strengths and weaknesses. The trick is in getting a working blend between them. See the exercise on page 15 to explore your organisation's emergent strategies.

Case study: all organisations are changing all the time

This table shows the emergent strategies of a youth agency. It describes how the agency's work was shaped by events, demands and external factors rather than a deliberate plan:

Emergent strategy: unplanned trend	Possible cause	Strategic issues
Less outreach work. Now only working with those who come to us.	Pressure of keeping the centre open for ten sessions – funder says that is what is important.	What balance should there be between centre-based and field work?
More in-depth work with fewer young people.	Two workers have trained in counselling and want to practise it.	Is this what we are supposed to be doing?
More young black women using the centre.	Possibly because we employed a woman worker who is black.	What would happen if she left?
More work with 13- to 16-year-olds.	Because older teenagers are into other things.	Who should be in our target group?
More time spent on fundraising.	Funders will not pay core costs.	Should we find better ways of making our case?
Doing more work on drug misuse.	Because there are funds available for this work.	How could this develop? Do we want to do more or less of this?

Strategic planning helps you to manage uncertainty and avoid short-termism

Political changes, annual budgets and short-term funding can make any notion of planning difficult, but there is a paradox about planning: the harder it is to plan, the more important clear planning becomes.

The one thing that is certain is that everything will remain uncertain. Finding secure and committed long-term funding is improbable and difficult to achieve. Political and economic stability is unlikely owing to continual reorganisations, friction between central and local government and a chronic shortage of funds. The profile and expectations of an organisation's service users are unlikely to become fixed. These uncertainties can cause voluntary organisations to lose longer-term perspective, become driven by short-term demands and only deal with what is urgent rather than what is important. Consequently, this can make a voluntary organisation's existence vulnerable.

During research for this book, a local authority officer with the responsibility for making grants to local voluntary groups said:

> Most of the organisations I deal with would be very easy to cut, and if cut, could close quickly. They are geared up from April to April and are fearful of taking on longer-term commitments. They employ their staff on short-term contracts (that in

practice are often renewed). They have no contingencies. They operate almost as if they expect to be closed down at a moment's notice.

Strategic planning is more and more about accepting uncertainty as a norm and having the confidence to chart a longer-term direction.

What can happen if you don't have a strategy

You become funder-led

Despite their best intentions, voluntary organisations frequently bid for and take on projects and activities because funding is available rather than because it meets their goals or needs. A trustee described how this was the case for his organisation: 'we've jumped on whatever funding bus happens to be passing – over the past few years we have been about detached youth work, counselling, drugs misuse prevention, social inclusion and now crime reduction. We have cut our cloth to fit whatever funders are into. As a result we have lost what we are about!'

The organisation turns into just a collection of projects

Many organisations have experienced a shift from being core funded to bidding for specific projects. The projects are usually fixed-term, and have their own identity within the organisation and sometimes little relationship to the other projects or activities in the organisation. As organisations move towards being project-based it is important that the host organisation has a clear direction and strategy that connects all the projects together.

You lose your vision and end up focused only on survival

In voluntary organisations where policy agendas change quickly, new structures, programmes and funding streams are launched and funding programmes rarely last beyond a few years, visions become increasingly short-term. Such turbulent change makes any long-term planning difficult as organisations jump from one issue to another. Short-term survival becomes the order of the day. By thinking strategically, you can go beyond the short-term perspective of some policy-makers and funders and ask questions such as what will happen after a fixed-term project ends? How will the organisation create lasting change rather than introducing temporary solutions? Good strategic thinking and planning can help to build a longer-term future and a sustainable organisation.

You feel unable to say 'no' to ideas, opportunities and demands

Trustees and workers can often feel guilty about saying 'no' to opportunities and ideas that could take the organisation to a new place. However, new ideas do need to be considered rationally and objectively. Do they really meet a need? Do you have the capacity to implement them? Are the risks manageable? Retaining a sense of the organisation's vision and mission and having a clear strategy helps an organisation to evaluate new ideas. It is the key to ensuring that the organisation keeps its integrity and purpose and avoids being sidetracked or jumping onto the passing bandwagon.

You want to be all things to all people

In any organisation there is a danger of trying to cover too many areas and spreading the organisation too thin. The Director of a local voluntary organisation expressed how this happens in her organisation: 'My organisation is brilliant at making priorities. We've got hundreds! Each time we have a planning meeting we get more.' Strategic planning is an opportunity to clarify the organisation's purpose, agree priorities and review activities. This can stop an organisation drifting or failing to deliver by trying to do too many things at once.

Your organisation's activities are only undertaken because you have always done them

Tradition and history play a part in any organisation. Precedents are set. Budgets and work plans are drawn up on the basis of the past year's performance. Once something is embedded in an organisation's structures and routines it can become a permanent fixture.

Setting a strategy gives you an opportunity and the time to review why you do things and challenge if they are the best way of using limited resources and energy.

Your organisational culture becomes resistant to change

A voluntary organisation can be a complex place. Often its workers have a relationship to it that is different from other workplaces: a personal or emotional relationship and commitment to the organisation's cause. This can be very positive, but can sometimes make change difficult and create contradictory situations. A worker in a campaigning organisation described this issue in her organisation: 'we have a very radical mission – as an organisation we are all about changing the world – but internally, it's different; simple changes like reducing the number of meetings are met with incredible resistance!'

Why bother writing a business plan?

The idea of producing a business plan can cause cynicism among staff. Indeed, there are several reasons which people can find to put off making one:

- Just continuing to operate on a day-to-day basis is enough of a struggle without the added stress of writing a plan that no one will use.
- The language of business planning is off-putting jargon.
- It is just another imported management fad that someone has picked up on a course.
- The word 'business' is objectionable, given that we are not commercial.
- It is difficult to plan during periods of constant change.
- It is daunting that the goal posts keep moving.
- We don't have enough skills or resources to implement the plan.

However, the reality is that organisations need not only to produce a credible plan but also to ensure that the plan feels real and relevant to people in the organisation. Whether it is called a business plan, a strategic plan or a forward plan is not important.

Here are some good reasons to write a business plan:

Funders require it

The tougher funding climate and the growth of a contract culture have led some funders and commissioners to require the production of a business plan before they consider a funding application. Business plans have their roots in the private sector and are an essential requirement in persuading lenders to back an enterprise. Some years ago now, like many other management concepts, they crossed from the profit-making sector to the voluntary sector.

Funders and business plans

Funders, commissioners and purchasers increasingly expect to see a business plan as part of the bidding process. Contact with a range of funders revealed six main issues that they expected to see addressed in the business plan:

1 To understand the idea behind the organisation or bid

The plan should set out the main idea behind the organisation. What is the vision that holds the organisation together? How is it different from others? It needs to set out a compelling picture of what the organisation is aiming to do and what it stands for.

2 To see that the plan has been fully worked out

Funders need convincing that an organisation's strategy and intentions have been thoroughly and objectively worked out. A secretary of a charitable foundation described how this is the case for his organisation: 'our funding panel increasingly wants to know that an organisation has properly thought through what it wants to do rather than being simply led by its interest or passion'.

3 To check that the organisation is being realistic

The plan needs to balance ambition and realism. All commitments and targets must be backed up with costings and measurable plans.

4 To ensure that the organisation has thought about possible risk

Every plan involves some sort of risk. A business plan needs to show that the main potential risks have been identified, analysed and that action has been taken to prevent them. The plan should show that the organisation has systems, processes and contingencies to prevent and monitor risks and enable it to act should they occur.

5 To check that the organisation has the capacity to deliver the plan

A programme manager for a government initiative commented that: 'plenty of organisations have brilliant ideas which are relevant and worthwhile, but the plan needs to convince us that the organisation has the management ability and experience to turn an idea into something that delivers'. The plan needs to show that the organisation has the systems, people and structures to manage properly.

6 To understand the longer-term picture

The plan needs to show that the organisation is not just going from one event or funding opportunity to another. It should show that as well as having short-term plans the organisation has a longer-term vision.

To create confidence in the organisation

Voluntary organisations can often suffer from a credibility gap. The outside world can see them as being made up of well-intentioned amateurs. Funders insist on rigorous and bureaucratic controls on how 'their' money is being spent. Sometimes this rubs off on the staff and volunteers who fail to see the effectiveness and efficiency of their efforts fully or that they are achieving incredible results with minimal resources. A central part of a business plan is to make the case for an organisation. It sets out the track record of the organisation, and demonstrates that it has effective systems, people and processes in place and that it can deliver results. Voluntary organisations are increasingly being called upon to show (through producing a business plan) that they will be a reliable partner in a contract or funding agreement. The process of drawing up a business plan can help an organisation to value itself more and to be more assertive with the outside world.

To help you keep a grip on reality

All too often, plans degenerate into a wish list of how we would like things to be in a perfect world or consist only of catchy mission statements without any real evidence that the organisation has worked out how to move forward. A proper business plan helps you to ensure that the realities of the organisation in its present situation are taken into account and sets out clear steps for its implementation.

Exercises

Throughout this book there is a range of exercises to help to develop the business planning process and also to present ideas and analysis in the plan itself. The techniques can be used in three different ways:

- at an individual level to clarify thinking and to start to develop ideas;
- in groups – management committee meetings, staff meetings and awaydays – to involve others in the process;
- in the plan itself – the completed exercise can be presented in the plan to show the analysis and thinking that led to the plan.

The following table provides a summary of all the exercises in the book. This should be useful for planning any training exercises needed during the strategic planning process or for awaydays and other events.

Exercise	Page	Objective
Making your strategy real	12	To find out what strategy means in your organisation and hence what changes may need to be made to your approach.
Why do you need a business plan?	13	To stimulate thinking about why you are involved in a business plan.
Emergent strategies: – how is your organisation changing?	15	To work out in which ways your organisation may be being pushed in a direction by unplanned forces.
Strategy – ten starter questions	24	To prime people to think about strategic issues in their organisation
Looking back to move forward	25	To help people think about and discuss how the organisation can evolve.

Exercise	Page	Objective
8 Signs of organisational complacency	27	An exercise to challenge the status quo.
Is there a need for strategic thinking?	28	To help establish a common sense of purpose about why strategic thinking is needed and to improve how it is approached.
Two approaches to strategy	37	To determine which type of approach to strategy is dominant in your organisation and to determine the best method.
Ten ways to mess up your organisation's strategic process	38	To review how your organisation really approaches the strategic process and hence to identify how to improve it.
Levels of involvement	48	To work out how your organisation currently consults and involves people in the process, the pros and cons of the method or methods used, and whether anything needs to change.
Consultation and decisions – how, who and when?	49	To consider who will give final approval to the plan and who will need to be consulted, then evaluate what they will contribute to the process and how and when they will be involved.
What if we did not exist?	68	To focus on the vision, purpose and role of your organisation.
Working out a mission statement	69	To aid the crafting of a mission statement.
Working out your values	70	To identify the key values or principles that should run through the organisation.
What roles do you play?	71	To review the different roles an organisation can play, how the organisation has evolved, whether the number of roles fulfilled is viable, and how these roles could develop in the future.
A SWOT analysis	96	To provide a snapshot analysis of the issues facing an organisation at a particular point and to identify which issues need to be tackled.
		This is useful as a starter exercise to encourage people to identify the issues and help share different people's perspectives. Needs to be followed up with action planning.
Predicting change	97	To identify the types of change facing the organisation.
Predicting trends and developments	98	To start the planning process by looking at outside developments, trends and external factors. Research on trends may need to be done.
Looking outside	99	To compare the organisation with organisations doing similar work and identify possible strategic avenues for cooperation, such as joint ventures and mergers.
Comparing resources and results	100	To show how your organisation allocates and uses resources in relation to its outcomes.
Your organisation's development stage	102	To identify your organisation's current stage of development and which organisational and management issues need to be tackled.

Exercise	Page	Objective
A portfolio matrix for your organisation	103	To analyse the value and balance of your organisation's activities or projects.
Comparing mission and activity	104	To help your organisation compare its activities (services, programmes and projects) with its intended purpose and mission.
Testing your assumptions	127	To identify and challenge the validity of the assumptions upon which the plan rests and work out what should happen if they do not work out as planned.
Managing new ideas and creating innovation	129	To review how creative your organisation is and to encourage innovative ideas.
Scenario planning	131	To provide an introduction to scenario planning.
Ideas prompt worksheet	132	To encourage individuals to identify strategic ideas, options and opportunities in their area of work.
Should we keep it going?	133	To consider the options available for dealing with a failing activity.
How clear is the direction?	134	To review how strong the strategic direction is by exploring how it would affect the organisation and its activities.
Strategy planner	135	To clarify the intention of a strategic goal, how its progress will be measured, which actions need to be taken and which costs will be involved.
A financial health check	165	To review financial processes, policies and procedures. It is important that this is not just left to the treasurer.
Predicting trends in current income	172	To look at the make-up of current income and how it might develop.
A trading venture checklist	173	To check that the ideas behind a trading venture have been fully worked out and to identify areas for further consideration.
Proving your track record	189	To show that the organisation has capacity to deliver the plan.
Mind the gap	192	To identify the changes that need to be made as a result of the plan.
Learning from the past: identifying critical success factors	193	A way of identifying critical success factors.
Developing critical success factors	195	To outline the actions which need to be taken to achieve the critical success factors, the associated key performance indicators and who holds overall responsibility for each critical success factor.
The elevator test	204	To check that everyone understands and can put forward the key messages of the plan.
Evaluating your plan	205	A final check to assess the plan.

✎ Exercise: making your strategy real

This brief exercise encourages you to think about how your organisation currently approaches strategy. It helps you to recognise where you are starting from and to work out where you need to go.

Mark the position of your organisation on each of these continuum lines. How does it measure up?

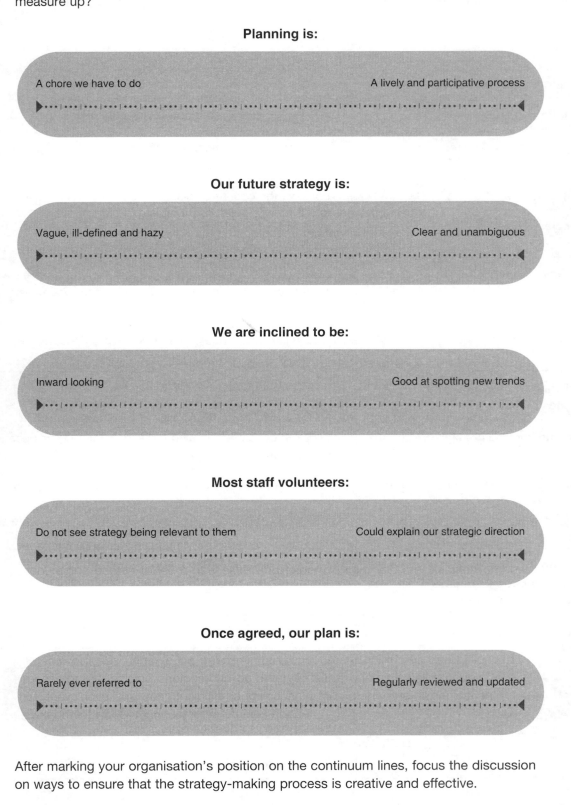

Planning is:

A chore we have to do   A lively and participative process

Our future strategy is:

Vague, ill-defined and hazy   Clear and unambiguous

We are inclined to be:

Inward looking   Good at spotting new trends

Most staff volunteers:

Do not see strategy being relevant to them   Could explain our strategic direction

Once agreed, our plan is:

Rarely ever referred to   Regularly reviewed and updated

After marking your organisation's position on the continuum lines, focus the discussion on ways to ensure that the strategy-making process is creative and effective.

✎ Exercise: why do you need a business plan?

This exercise aims to encourage you and your colleagues to be clear about why you are involved in a business planning process. Take a moment before you start to think about how you can make it a useful exercise for your organisation. You may want to add, for example, other external and internal motivations.

Which of the following reasons are important to you? In the boxes provided overleaf, score them on a scale of 1 to 4.

Rating:

1: No/little importance
2: Some importance
3: Important
4: Very important

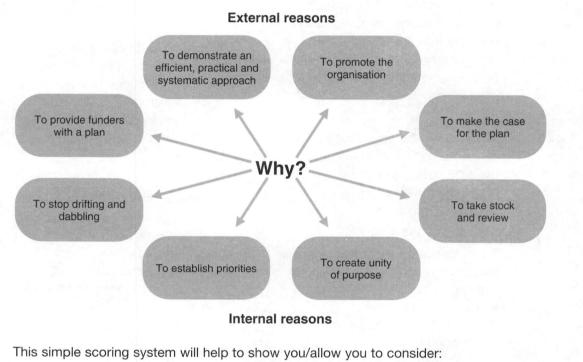

External reasons

To demonstrate an efficient, practical and systematic approach

To promote the organisation

To provide funders with a plan

To make the case for the plan

Why?

To stop drifting and dabbling

To take stock and review

To establish priorities

To create unity of purpose

Internal reasons

This simple scoring system will help to show you/allow you to consider:

● the main factors that will motivate people to go ahead with the process;
● what a business plan will enable you to do,
● how a business plan will be used;
● how to balance external and internal forces;
● how a business plan can make your organisation stronger.

External

☐ **To provide funders with a plan:** a good plan helps to make the case for the organisation. It helps funders to understand the organisation and feel confident about backing and supporting it. It sets out your stall and allows funders to consider what you're offering.

☐ **To demonstrate an efficient, practical and systematic approach:** voluntary organisations need to show that they are managed properly. A business plan can demonstrate that there is good and efficient management in place which will ensure that the plan is delivered and funds are used properly.

☐ **To promote the organisation:** the plan is one of the ways of marketing the organisation by explaining the idea, vision and strategies to funders and others.

☐ **To make the case for the plan:** the plan can show how ideas and aspirations can be turned into a reality. It helps people to understand the context and background.

Internal

☐ **To stop drifting and dabbling:** it is easy to get pulled in many directions at once. A good business plan will help to create clarity about direction and ensure that the organisation's goals are realistic.

☐ **To establish priorities:** it is not possible for everything to be equally important. Organisations need to decide where and how to focus their efforts; this will include saying 'no' to some ideas, opportunities and requests.

☐ **To create unity of purpose:** the process can bring trustees, staff and volunteers together. Building a shared vision of what you want to do and the strategy for doing it can be a valuable team-building exercise.

☐ **To take stock and review:** a plan needs to be based on an appraisal of what you do now. The plan can provide an opportunity to challenge how you do things, evaluate programmes and have a rethink.

You need to balance the internal and external reasons for making the plan. Too much emphasis on the external reasons can lead to a plan that is really only written to get money from funders. Too much emphasis on internal reasons can lead to the process being too inward-looking: the organisation fails to see external opportunities or is not prepared for changes that could influence or even threaten its future.

✎ Exercise: emergent strategies – how is your organisation changing?

It is useful to ask participants in the planning process to reflect on the past few years and to try to identify what sorts of direction the organisation has moved in and is currently moving in. The discussion should focus on what has driven the organisation, what has controlled it and what choices have been made subconsciously by individuals and teams.

Emergent strategy: unplanned trend	Possible cause	Strategic issues

Which things does your organisation need to be deliberate about?

How do you create space in your plan to respond to opportunities that emerge?

Chapter two
Strategic thinking

'Strategic' is an impressive-sounding word but it is overused to the point that it can become meaningless. If ever you need to make an issue sound more complex and considered, put the word strategic in front of it: 'strategic problem' or 'strategic issue' or 'strategic role' suddenly sound a lot cleverer than the simple terms alone.

Different definitions of strategy abound. Many have their roots in military thinking and developing tactics to win battles. Quotes from the likes of Sun Tzu, the ancient Chinese leader on the art of war, might be interesting or even inspiring, but are hard to apply to a voluntary organisation which is coping with increased demand and declining resources. Equally, what might work in a profit-making business might not easily make the transfer to a voluntary organisation.

Strategy can be defined simply as what you have to do to accomplish what you want to achieve. There are many more academic definitions out in the world, but this is a practical book and so this chapter focuses on the thinking aspect of strategy and aims to show what strategic thinking is in practice. In particular, it outlines how you can encourage people to think and act in a strategic way both when things are good and during more difficult times.

How to think strategically

Strategic thinking cannot be switched on like a light bulb. It needs time, support and processes. People are often so busy coping with day-to-day events and demands that they find no time to think about or work on the strategic issues. How often does creative thinking happen when you are away from work? Strategic thinking should not be the role of one or two people in an organisation. The results of the strategic process have the potential to involve everyone in an organisation, so surely it is sensible that many people are involved and engaged in the thinking that puts the strategy together.

Here are some approaches and activities that can help to encourage strategic thinking either individually or in groups.

Be willing and able to challenge the obvious

For strategic work to be effective, permission needs to be given to question and challenge the way things are. This might mean being able to question the explicit and implicit decisions and assumptions that underpin how your organisation operates. In most organisations or groups there are issues that are never properly tackled or formally spoken about. For example, the long-standing fundraising activity that costs more to run than it brings in, or the service that takes up lots of time but does not really deliver an outcome. The strategic process should be an opportunity to constructively challenge and question issues that are often avoided or ignored.

See the bigger system

It is easy to become inward-looking and not see in which ways the world outside has an impact on your organisation. However, this tendency must be overcome to allow you to see how your organisation connects to a bigger system – how the decisions, roles and activities of others affect your development. Doing this can prevent people from feeling isolated and it can help you to identify ways of increasing the impact your organisation makes by playing a more active part in the bigger system.

Be positive and confident

It is easy for the realities of organisational management to depress and grind a person down. Insecurity, funding gaps, short-termism and competing demands can create a negative and depressing atmosphere that dominates the process. It is important to recognise the negative factors and get beyond them to allow people to be optimistic, creative and innovative about future prospects. This requires what the Italian political thinker, Antonio Gramsci, described as 'pessimism of the intellect, optimism of the will'. Sometimes it is necessary to rekindle the vision and sense of purpose that were there when the organisation began and at key points in its history.

Understand the past to move forward

Looking at your organisation's history can help to explain the way it is now and identify trends, cycles and factors that keep reoccurring. To move forward it is useful to know where you have come from and recognise the organisation's continual evolution. The following case study demonstrates a practical format for doing this.

Case study: looking back to move forward

The staff, volunteers and trustees of a community development centre used this exercise to start their strategic planning day. The final sheet looked like this:

The past: how the organisation was when you first came into contact with it	The present: how the organisation is now	The future: how the organisation will need to be
• Exciting	• Bigger	• Higher-profile
• Small	• Recognised	• Still focused
• No systems or procedures	• Challenging	• Strong image and identity
• Strong focus on vision	• Strategic	• More diverse membership
• Lots of local people involved	• Own identity	• More diverse income
• Organised chaos	• Clear profile	• Contracted to deliver more diverse services
• Flexible	• Organised, results-driven and focused	• Working in partnership with others
• Unique	• Professional but still friendly	• Independent
• Full of ideas	• We deliver results	• Social enterprise
• Patchy	• Some skills lacking	• Campaigning
• Friendly	• Uncertainty about the future	• Influential
• Social	• Emphasis on paid staff	• Local people and local service users involved
• A 'family atmosphere'	• Has systems and procedures	• Sustainable
• Dependent on Jane as founder	• Bureaucratic	• Recognised
• Everyone was involved in everything	• Less involvement of local people	• Thick-skinned
• Conflicts with council	• Committed	• Efficient
	• Better relations with council	• Expert
		• Show our value

Which things have you been doing that you need to keep doing?

We need to continue being efficient, systematic and able to win contracts and at the same time remain responsive to local people.

Which things do you want to rekindle?

We need to ensure that as we grow we remain innovative, willing to take risks and open to new ideas and requests from local people.

How big a change will it be to move from what you're doing now to what you want to do in the future?

Social enterprise, working in partnerships and generating income will require a new focus and some new skills. May also require new skills on our management committee.

Which future elements could you start now?

We could start by developing and testing our ideas for social enterprise and also identify who we might want to partner with.

What kind of culture do you want to build?

We need a culture that supports innovation, risk taking and is entrepreneurial in our approach to new opportunities and needs. At the same time we have to be led by local people and not become just another agency with its own agenda. We must be practical and able to deliver things that make a real change.

To try this exercise in your organisation, see page 25.

Overcoming people's anxieties about strategic planning

Introducing strategic planning often involves overcoming people's objections and anxieties about it. Here are some common objections to the process and how they can be challenged:

'Times are too uncertain to plan'

While the constant state of uncertainty and flux of funding programmes, political directions and other factors make it feel very difficult to create a strategy, a strong strategy is crucial to prevent an organisation drifting and to create direction.

'What's the point of developing a strategy if it cannot be funded?'

Too much focus on funding can lead to an organisation becoming funder-led: it loses its own identity and direction and simply chases after whatever funding is available. A strategic process is an opportunity to set your stall out for funders and commissioners and help them to understand your role and potential.

'We are too busy – we don't have time for it.'

Strategic planning will take time. You need to schedule time for when you are going to plan to ensure that the process is organised and uses people's time wisely. In some instances the lack of a strategy and a clear plan to support it can lead to an organisation taking on too many activities and being pulled in too many directions. A good strategy should help to focus the organisation on what's important and ensure that time is spent on what matters.

'We are OK as we are – why can't we stay as we are?'

The strategic process does not mean that everything has to change for the sake of it. However, it does provide an opportunity to ensure that what you do is still relevant, to see how you might be affected by external change and to guard against complacency.

'It might raise difficult issues.'

Looking at your organisation might bring to the surface weaknesses, gaps and simmering conflicts. This could be uncomfortable and disruptive. Clearly these issues need careful handling, but surely it is better to deal with them in a deliberate way, as they are unlikely to disappear on their own.

Managers and strategic thinking

To work at a strategic level, managers may need to develop some additional skills. Most management time is spent on supervising or running things; working at a strategic level can involve shifting into a different gear. Based on experience of working in and with different organisations, I would suggest that managers need the following attributes to work at a strategic level:

- **A capacity to see and explain the bigger picture:** the ability to explain how the different activities of the organisation connect together and fit into an overall vision. This is particularly important when organisations become more complex and diverse.

- **An ability to look outside:** the capacity to spot new developments, trends and emerging opportunities.

- **A fresh or challenging perspective**: an ability to think creatively, challenge the existing way of doing things and introduce new ideas and skills that can stimulate the process and combat complacency or an inward-looking, defensive culture.

- **An ability to deal with change:** the skills needed to communicate ideas, plan change and cope with the anxiety and uncertainty that occur in periods of change.

- **The quality of persistence:** the ability to stick with a new strategy and support it when the going gets tough can be the key to implementation. Managers need to know when to push a strategy and ensure that it does not get derailed.

Case study: being too close to the organisation

The director of a health charity described how he struggled to be strategic:

I spend my days rushing from one thing to another. My role should be strategic, but it ends up being mainly reactive. I realise that I spend so much time here that I have lost perspective. At times I get so involved in the detail that I miss the bigger picture.

I have tried to work on this. I now know that I can be so involved in the organisation that I fail to think creatively about its future direction. This year I have been very fortunate in having two new trustees who are very good at challenging me, occasionally stretching my thinking (often by asking awkward and obvious questions) and bringing a fresh outside perspective to our discussions.

I've found that to operate at a strategic level you need to stand back a little and be a bit detached.

Strategic thinking in hard times

It is much easier to strategise and plan when things are good. In recent years the context and climate in which we plan has become more challenging: funding is in short supply, austerity, cutbacks and uncertainty are the order of the day and competition between organisations has increased. As service users and communities experience hard times, demand for services is on the increase and at the same time resources decline. Organisations are optimistically and naively encouraged to 'do more with less'.

Common responses during these difficult times include:

● ignoring the issue until it becomes a crisis;
● overreacting: refusing to spend any money, closing programmes and general panic and crisis management;
● chasing after any funding that is going: redoubling funding and bidding work to go after any funding regardless of its appropriateness or the implications of taking it on;
● and the classic response: 'something will turn up – it always does'.

Uncertainty, anxiety and stress all work against the need to think ahead and manage proactively. It is very easy to fall into the trap of becoming entirely focused on crisis management and short-term survival to the extent that medium- to longer-term opportunities and possibilities are ignored or disregarded.

Responding to these factors and being able to think through them strategically requires a different approach and needs a clear leadership.

Case study: beyond crisis

The manager of a youth work charity described the issues he faced in trying to cope in increasingly tough times:

Just before the start of the new financial year we go through a weird annual ritual. As manager I deliver a report to trustees on future funding prospects. For the past three years the report has become increasingly depressing – public sector cutbacks, a much tougher fundraising climate and greater competition. Our trustees then spend an hour looking awkward and gloomy. Ideas on what to do are limited to 'let's work harder at fundraising' or 'this happens every year and something always turns up'. The unspoken assumption is that I as the manager will find some way of coping. Magician-like, I will keep finding rabbits to pull out of hats. In many ways this is understandable. We have managed to find ways of getting by against all the odds. We have moved money about, grabbed hold of any funding that is going and just about managed to keep the organisation afloat.

We have got to find a way to look at the issue strategically rather than lurching from one crisis to the next. My view is that we need to ask some serious questions about what our priorities are and where we should put our increasingly limited resources. I think we need to look critically at how we are organised. We have fairly large overhead costs for a relatively small organisation. We also need to test out if we can collaborate and even merge with similar agencies as a way to make us stronger.

A key task for me is to create the space and time for our trustees and staff to look at future strategy before we get to the next recurring crisis.

Managing in tough times – a strategic approach

- **Make sure that the organisation's vision and mission are clear, relevant and understood.** A clear sense of purpose should give your organisation's leadership some clarity when it tackles difficult decisions. Clarity of vision and mission should help to retain a sense of independence and create unity within the organisation and can help to avoid becoming led only by available funding. See Chapter 5 for help on how to review or set a vision and mission.

- **Analyse what you do.** It is important to be clear about which of your organisation's activities are core and which are secondary.

- **Collect and show evidence.** It is no longer good enough to do 'good work' – you now need to be able to demonstrate it and show it. Funders and commissioners increasingly pose challenging questions asking organisations to show that they make a real difference or deliver particular outcomes. A lot of performance measurement systems still report on how busy an organisation is at the output level (we gave 120 hours of advice) rather than reporting the outcomes (20 clients are now settled in permanent accommodation). Find ways of recording and analysing the outcomes.

- **Ask questions.** Should the organisation continue business as usual or is a new model needed? Is the problem that you are experiencing a temporary blip or is it a longer-term problem? Have you just been unlucky in failing to attract sufficient funding or has the landscape changed so much that you need a different model and strategy?

- **Turn outwards and build alliances.** Turn around the tendency to turn inwards and become defensive. Now might be the time to explore ways of working with organisations that have a similar role or mission to yours. Might there be potential in looking at forms of collaboration such as alliances, joint working, joint ventures or even mergers as a way of strengthening your future position?

- **Communicate like never before.** People in and around the organisation need to know what is happening. Sharing your plans, asking for support and preparing people for change may help the process and stop the organisation or the people in it from becoming isolated.

- **Be ready for change.** Ensure that your organisation is ready for change: that systems, processes and procedures are in good shape. The organisation may need to make decisions quickly, consult staff and work through demanding staffing issues such as redeployment, job change or redundancy. It is important that policies and procedures for such issues are in place and in workable order before you need them.

- **Revisit your market.** Now might be a good time to reconnect with your service users or the communities that you are there to benefit. How have their needs changed? What do they want from you? Which opportunities might emerge?

- **Plan and manage the finances**. In tough times your ability to control and monitor your finances may be tested. Cash flow management and forecasting needs to be a regular and continual activity rather than an occasional event. You may need an early-warning system to alert you to business problems ahead.

- **Be in control.** Be clear about who can make decisions and what the process is for involvement and consultation. Endlessly talking about a problem is unlikely to change it. At times you may need to make decisions and act quickly. See Chapter 4 for advice on good consultation.

Exercise: strategy – ten starter questions

These questions are designed to get participants in a strategic thinking mindset.

Question	Prompts	Follow-up discussion:
What were we set up to achieve?	• What was the original idea behind the organisation? • Is it still relevant? • Does it still inspire us?	• Do we understand the overall vision and mission? • Are they still relevant?
If we were starting out today what would we do differently?	• What have we learnt? • What's changed?	• Do we need to change our vision, mission and values?
What do we feel passionate about or committed to?	• What inspires us? • What would success for the organisation look like in three to five years' time?	• How do we generate a shared commitment to a core purpose?
What do other people think of us?	• How would others describe us? • How do the people who matter to us rate what we do?	• What feedback do we need? • Can we use their ideas in the strategic process?
What are we good at?	• Which activities do we do well? • What skills and expertise do we have within the organisation?	• What do we do better than others? What's our competitive advantage? • Should we do more of what we are good at?
Over the next few years what are the main external factors we need to consider?	• What is happening in our community/market or sector that we need to respond to? • What trends and factors will influence our future?	• How well in touch with our external environment are we? • What's happening out there?
What ideas do we have that need developing?	• What ideas for new projects, services or activities do we want to consider further?	• How can the organisation encourage creative ideas and innovation?
Who has got a stake or an interest in our future development?	• Who might have something to contribute to our planning process? • Whose support and goodwill might we need to implement the plan?	• How can we best involve them in the strategic process?
Can we stay the same?	• Do we need to change? • What internal and external factors are changing around us?	• What is driving the change? • What's the risk in staying as we are?
Are there any ideas we can steal or borrow?	• What are other people doing? • What's new in our sector?	• How do we keep ahead of our game?

Exercise: looking back to move forward

This exercise is designed to help you think about and discuss how your organisation might continue to evolve and change. It is simple but can help you to see patterns and understand why organisations need to develop and respond continually to changes.

Ask participants to describe the organisation in three timeframes as shown in the following table. In each column they should think about and describe:

- the organisation;
- the prevailing culture, atmosphere and style;
- the focus: key priorities and direction.

Two things are important to consider in this process. First, everyone has a different perception based on time, experience and their role. Second, sometimes it is easier and clearer to use short words or gut feelings to describe things rather than more complex descriptions. See page 19 for an example of the short descriptions another organisation used when completing this exercise.

The past: how it was when they first came into contact with it	The present: how it is now	The future: how it will need to be

Once individuals have completed their own exercise, the group can go on to compare their statements and try to spot key themes. To help steer the discussion usefully, they can focus on the following questions:

What are the key things currently driving the organisation?

Which things have you been doing that you need to keep doing?

Which things do you want to rekindle?

How big a change will it be to move from what you're doing now to what you want to do in the future?

Which future elements could you start now?

What kind of culture do you want to build?

Exercise: eight signs of organisational complacency

Organisational complacency is when an organisation turns inward and stops developing and thinking strategically. Sometimes it can produce organisational blind spots or even a collective arrogance. Changing and trying to do new things is hard work.

Here are eight signs of organisational complacency. Try this exercise to see if you recognise any of these signs in your organisation, and hence identify in which areas you need to make changes, work harder or any you need to keep an eye on.

Score the following statements on the following scale.

Rating:

1: We do this frequently
2: We sometimes do this
3: We rarely do this
4: This never applies to us

Organisational approach
Rating

1. We rarely ask other people what they think of us. We don't receive and hardly ever look for feedback or comments from people outside our organisation.

2. We rarely spend time looking for new needs and spotting external trends. We do very little research or work on identifying new trends that could have an impact on us.

3. We are very comfortable with how we are. There is a strong sense that we like what we do and are satisfied with it.

4. Our usual first response is to avoid or resist change. We can be defensive in reacting to new ideas and change.

5. We often fall into carrying out projects in an unplanned way. We frequently have to run to catch up with new developments.

6. The general view in the organisation is that we are the best at what we do. People feel that we are always good at what we do.

7. Lots of things happen because that's how we did it in the past. We operate by routines and precedents.

8. We rarely evaluate properly or challenge what we do. We don't often make time to question or rethink what we do.

🖎 Exercise: is there a need for strategic thinking?

The following eight statements were made by a group of managers about to embark on a strategic planning exercise. Do any of the sentiments expressed sound like those voiced in your organisation?

1. 'We have grown far too fast. Some parts of the organisation are now disconnected from each other.'

2. 'We are drifting. The past few years all our energy has been spent on keeping going. We need to establish a new direction.'

3. 'We need to establish a common sense of purpose and direction that will hold the project together.'

4. 'We could be criticised for trying to be all things to all people. We need to sort out our identity and make priorities.'

5. 'The need for our services is growing fast, the resources to meet that need are declining. We are in danger of becoming a crisis-driven, 'first aid' service.'

6. 'We have been so busy managing that we have missed out on several opportunities to develop new initiatives.'

7. 'I have trouble explaining to outsiders what the organisation is for.'

8. 'We are in danger of becoming complacent and inward-looking. We cannot assume that what we are doing now will be the same in two years' time.'

How would you describe the current state of strategic thinking in your organisation?

Who does strategic thinking in your organisation and where does it happen?

How could it be improved?

Chapter three
The planning process

Every organisation is different in that it faces its own particular challenges and works in different settings. This means that a strategy cannot be simply picked off the shelf or copied from elsewhere. Nevertheless, as outlined in Chapter 1, all organisations are going somewhere: the future direction may be about the organisation getting bigger or smaller, working in a different way or doing more or less of a particular activity. The important thing is, whatever the organisation and its distinctiveness, that the process is carried out well, because how the process is managed and how people are involved in it have a considerable bearing on the result.

This chapter outlines the process as a whole and the stages within it, demonstrating what must be done to make an effective strategy in practice.

Getting things in order: the planning process in outline

It is important to get things into a logical order. Figure 3.1 sets out an outline process map for the strategic and business planning process.

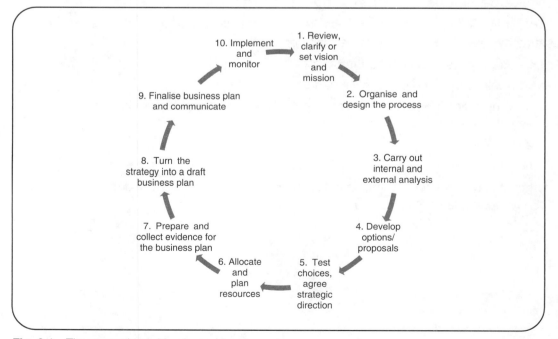

Fig. 3.1 The strategic and business planning process

1. Purpose: agree the overall vision and mission

This is about checking or updating the overriding vision and mission that should underpin and give meaning to everything the organisation does. The vision and mission must help people to understand the point of what the organisation is trying to achieve. They should connect all activities and projects and give the whole organisation (and the rest of the plan) a sense of purpose.

Discussions should be about answering some fundamental questions, such as:

● What is our overall purpose?

● What is the big idea behind the organisation/what do we stand for?

● What are we trying to achieve?

● Who do we exist for?

● What are our values?

Clarity about these questions should provide an anchor for the process. Chapter 5 considers in full this stage of the process.

2. Approach: design the process

The process by which the plan is developed and prepared has a critical impact on its successful implementation. Most of us have had enough experience of plans that create reams of paper and lead to no action, and this sort of experience leads us to hesitance or cynicism about the planning process. Therefore, it is worthwhile investing time in the process and thinking about how people's time can be best used and ensuring that they feel committed to planning. The following points can aid the organisation of the process:

Make time

Organisations need to carve out time for strategic thinking and planning. The hardest and worst kind of organisational planning comes when it is too late; this is when planning becomes entirely reactive or is focused on crisis management. To be effective you need to aim to be ahead of the game; i.e. you need to identify issues before they become urgent and think proactively about how you want the organisation to develop.

Make decisions on the strategic management process

The strategic management process itself is crucially important for the success of a strategy. Decisions will need to be made on:

● the key stages of preparing the plan;

● who will be involved or consulted and at which stage;

● how the process will fit around other established management procedures (such as setting the budget);

● a timetable for the process;

● how the strategy will be communicated;

● how the strategy will be implemented, monitored and evaluated and how change will be managed (see Chapter 11).

Agree objectives for the strategic and business plan

The task of agreeing objectives for the strategic and business plan can help to clarify the internal and external reasons why a plan is needed and to show why time should be taken to create a strategy.

Although it is probably much better to work out your own possible objectives for the plan, they might include:

- To develop a realistic future strategy
- To clarify long-term aims
- To relate all activities to the aims
- To make measurable plans
- To link future developments in the external environment to internal change
- To convince financial backers that the organisation is credible

Set up a planning group

You can set up a sub-group to lead the planning process. The group needs to be focused on the tasks and have the relevant skills and insights to drive the process. Be careful it does not become an endless series of meetings. To mitigate this potential problem the group can set out some terms of reference, which describe the purpose and objectives of the group, who is involved and to whom they are accountable, and how the objectives will be achieved. The following box outlines a draft terms of reference for a planning group.

Hire a consultant

An external consultant can facilitate the process, bring a new or challenging perspective and provide expert guidance. It is important that the consultant is well briefed and understands the context and nature of your organisation. The consultant can only aid the process – the responsibility for implementation and ownership of the plan must be with the organisation's leadership.

✎ Example: draft terms of reference for a strategy group

Terms of Reference

Strategy group: appointed and accountable to the board of trustees

Made up of: Deputy Chief Officer, HR Officer, Vice Chair of Trustees, Southern Area Manager, Volunteer Development Officer and Funding Officer

Reporting to the trustees through the Director.

A task group: to meet four times and complete its task by the June board meeting.

Objectives:

- To design, coordinate and lead the process of developing the organisation's future strategy.
- To design and manage a planning process that involves staff, volunteers, service users and other stakeholders in the planning process and delivers a plan for the approval of the board of trustees that is clear, realistic and sound.
- To recruit, appoint and brief an external consultant who will design and facilitate a planning day to start the process, engage people in thinking strategically and develop and explore future options.
- To gather relevant data, evidence of trends and feedback that will help to inform the process, explain the context in which we are operating and influence our decisions.
- To actively consult the service user group, key funders and commissioners to ensure that they are able to feed into the process.
- To identify the key options open to the organisation.
- To develop and present to the trustees' April meeting an initial report setting out key issues and suggesting outline strategic goals for the board's amendment and approval.
- To coordinate a process after the April meeting whereby team leaders and managers work with their staff and volunteer teams to produce operational plans and budgets to show how their work will develop and change in the light of the strategic goals.
- To oversee the drafting of a full plan based on the strategic goals and team plans and to work with the management team and finance manager to ensure that the plan is fully costed, robust and realistic.
- To present the plan for approval to the June trustees' meeting.
- To make any amendments to the plan in the light of the trustees' meeting.
- To work with the management team to agree a process to ensure that the plan is communicated throughout the organisation and is monitored and updated.
- To produce a review of this process against the original objectives highlighting lessons learned.

3. Analysis: internal and external

This stage should help to make the planning process a more informed one. It should ensure that before agreeing a future direction, everyone involved has a sound understanding of the issues facing the organisation both internally and externally.

Internal factors

First, look at how the organisation has developed internally. Work at this stage should include gathering and sharing information about the current state of the organisation. This involves pulling together information about what the organisation does currently and appraising services and activities against the need and the organisation's purpose. It is also an opportunity to review what is and is not working and gather feedback from people with an interest or stake in the organisation.

External factors

Second, look outside the organisation to recognise how the external context is changing. This involves looking at how the landscape for the organisation is developing and spotting trends that could have an impact on what you do. This is about trying to predict and anticipate changes that could have an effect on the organisation: the issues identified may be opportunities or threats. It is also about being able to create opportunities by seeing how things are developing, rather than by falling into situations in an unplanned way. A key decision in the strategic process, therefore, is recognising which external factors you need to respond to.

Chapter 6 elaborates on this part of the process in full.

4. Options: developing ideas

At this stage, ideas about how the organisation could develop should be actively pursued; it should be a creative and challenging time. It is important to encourage fresh and innovative ideas and develop a range of options for the future development of the organisation. Participants should be encouraged to be bold and innovative in their ideas and not be constrained by how things are now or by concerns about funding and resources.

5. Strategic direction: choices and testing

Once the options have been identified, they need to be debated and evaluated against the criteria of which ones are most likely to help you to achieve your vision. This stage is about focus and direction, agreeing what the organisation's priorities will be and what role the organisation should play. It is about establishing and focusing on an achievable number of key goals that the organisation will commit to in the medium term to advance its mission, i.e. setting out how the organisation should use its limited resources to achieve its purpose.

It can be very tempting to say 'yes' to all interesting and worthwhile ideas even though they are not really priorities. The list of 'priorities' ends up growing to unrealistic and unhelpful proportions. To mitigate this tendency, different tests should be used to consider each option, such as clarifying your position by answering the following sorts of questions:

- Does it fit with our vision and mission?
- Is it needed?
- Are we the best organisation to undertake it?
- What risks are involved?

Answering these can help your organisation to decide which ones to run with and which ones to reject. This requires a disciplined approach.

In summary, the critical elements of this stage are:

- agreeing what the organisation is not going to do as well as what it is going to do;
- ensuring that the number of priorities is realistic;
- balancing existing and new work.

See Chapter 7 for a full consideration of this part of the process.

6. Operational planning: allocating and planning resources

Once the strategic direction has been agreed the detailed planning work can start. This stage is about:

1. the detail of how the organisation will (or can) attract or earn the funds to do what it wants to do and deliver the strategy;
2. the organisation's structure and the best way to organise resources to deliver the strategy.

All of the organisation's resources (people, money and materials) need to be managed to ensure that they are being used to deliver the strategy or support the activities that fit with the organisation's strategic focus and support the delivery process. Each service or project needs to be fully costed. The costs involved in properly managing the organisation – i.e. the overheads – must be included. Once the costs have been agreed, they need to be compared against agreed, likely and possible incomes. This process usually requires some adjusting of the plan to fit with income projections.

This part of the process is considered more fully in Chapter 8.

7. Evidence: establishing credibility

This part of the process is about demonstrating that the organisation's historical and current performance has been properly evaluated to create the best plan for the future and hence make the case for why an organisation should receive support. Smaller organisations or new initiatives need to show that sufficient feasibility work on the plans has been carried out. Evidence needs to be collected to show that the organisation has a history of sound practice and good management and the right systems, structures and personnel to implement the plan. This involves identifying how people's roles may need to change to deliver the strategy and hence the additional skills required, and looking at how (and even if) existing staff can be supported to develop the requisite expertise. The organisation's structure may also need to change to support the strategy better. Management systems and processes should be checked to ensure best practice and that risks are minimised. Any potential risks identified should be shown to have been considered and actions to avoid them proposed.

This stage in the process is an opportunity for the organisation to market its expertise, skills and competence positively.

This stage is outlined in full in Chapter 9.

8. The document: writing the business plan

This stage is about turning the strategy into a written document. The plan needs to meet the needs of different audiences. External parties, such as potential and existing funders, must receive a clear message from the plan that helps them to understand the aspirations and intentions of the organisation and also to feel confident in the ability of the organisation to deliver them. Internally, trustees and staff should draw a clear understanding from the plan of the organisation's direction and priorities and how they fit in. Once the plan has been written it will need to be taken to the trustee board for approval. Revisions may be suggested.

This part of the process is considered more fully in Chapter 10.

9. Finalising and communicating the plan

Once any revisions have been made and the plan has been finally approved, this is when the document becomes a tool which can be used externally as well as internally. Internally, this plan should be used to help your organisation to know what it is trying to achieve and to have a clear focus on this. The priorities should be clear and individuals should be able to look at the strategy and see how their role and their contribution fit into the overall picture. Externally, the plan can help interested parties to understand the organisation's vision better and hence increase the chances of their support for the organisation.

10. Implementation and monitoring

This stage is about making the plan a reality and dealing with the changes that it will create. These can be changes in how you organise, what you do or how you operate. A key part of the strategy is to ensure that these changes are happening and will be sustained. You will need to think about the short- to longer-term implementation of the plan and the monitoring of its progress.

This part of the process is elaborated on in Chapter 11.

Getting things in the wrong order

The first response to a new project is to question how it will be paid for and whether existing or potential funders will support it. As we have noted, organisations sometimes do things not because they want to or because they are in line with their vision, but rather because there is funding available. It is important, therefore, to be vigilant about this common pitfall. Any organisation needs first to ensure that it is clear about what it wants to do and then look for ways of resourcing and funding it. Obviously if a strategy cannot be funded it needs to be reconsidered, but the alternative scenario is an organisation chasing after any possible funding and in doing so losing any sense of its identity or purpose.

Case study: the planning in process in a larger organisation

A national charity which employs nearly 150 staff working in six different functional teams throughout the UK developed a five-stage process to produce an organisational plan, as shown in figure 3.2 (note that this does not include the post-planning activities such as implementation).

The process started with organisation-wide planning that involved staff from throughout the charity looking at the overall development and role of the organisation and the options open to it. After this consultation the charity's trustees and senior managers finalised the wording of the vision and mission and set out six key strategic goals for the next three to five years.

Organisational and project teams were then asked to draw up their plans in a way that reflected the organisation's vision and agreed goals. Individual senior managers worked with the teams to ensure that plans were aligned to the organisational strategy. Once the team plans were agreed, they were collated into a single document.

Organisation-wide planning
Review and analysis of the organisation's overall vision, mission and future options

Agreement of vision and overall strategy
Leadership team agrees/updates vision and mission, and sets strategic direction

Team/project planning
Units develop their plans in line with the overall direction

Coordination
Discussion to ensure that unit plans are in line with the strategy

Agreement
Production of overall organisational plan

Fig. 3.2 A five-stage process

Exercise: two approaches to strategy

What does strategy mean in your organisation? What sort of strategist are you? By considering the following approaches – one focusing on the side of detail, order and control and the other on a spontaneous, responsive and creative approach – see which style is dominant in your organisation. Consider the pros and cons of both approaches and think about how you can get the best from both.

	Strategy as a controlled and systematic process	*Strategy as a responsive and creative process*
The emphasis is on:	● the detail	● rethinking the organisation's purpose and direction
The result is:	● a clear document that sets out exactly what the organisation intends to do	● an ongoing process that creates a united sense of direction
The content is about	● numbers, projections, data and tight objectives	● evaluation, ideas, reflection and clarity of purpose
The process involves:	● senior management setting the direction – individuals then write their objectives or work plan	● everyone participating in reviewing where the organisation is at, looking at trends and developing goals
The style is:	● about producing a professional and impressive plan	● a chance to stand back from what the organisation does, rethink and work out how to develop
The process is driven by:	● funders wanting it to happen, and a need to be efficient, practical and systematic	● a need to review where the organisation is and be clear where it is going
The focus is on	● detailed plans, budgets, work plans and timescales.	● clarity about our intended direction and how we can best move forward

Exercise: ten ways to mess up your organisation's strategic process

Rate each of these approaches to strategy depending on how much each one rings true (or not) for your organisation. Those you rate 1 or 2 are the areas you will need to focus on improving.

Rating:

1: We do this frequently
2: We sometimes do this
3: We rarely do this
4: This never applies to us

Organisational approach		Your rating 1–4
1. Base all plans on what we did in the past.	The plan is based on past work: how we operated and budgeted in recent years. It's a statement of history rather than a future plan.	
2. Start the process by working out how much money we have.	Finance and funding dominate all thinking. The plan is purely driven by finance.	
3. Strategy is achieved once we have written the final draft of the plan.	The whole focus is on producing a fine-looking document that few people will ever refer to or use again.	
4. Subject every new idea to rigorous investigation and analysis.	Any new creative idea or proposal has to be watertight and able to stand up to cross-examination.	
5. Don't even think about doing things that are risky.	The organisation prefers to do things that are safe, reliable and risk-free.	
6. Only managers in the organisation get to execute the plan.	The plan arrives from on high. The people who have to deliver it or the people who it is supposed to benefit were not involved in putting it together.	
7. The creation of the strategy is an internal process – there is no need to involve others.	The people running the organisation know best. What's the point of asking stakeholders to contribute?	
8. Encourage lots of ideas, new thinking and creativity throughout the process.	The process is a free-for-all. Ideas, fresh thinking and innovations are all generated, but never followed through.	
9. Strategy is all about the big-picture issues.	The plan is all about longer-term visions, aspirations and blue-sky thinking. It is idealistic and is not grounded in day-to-day realities.	
10. Once agreed, we have to stick to it.	The plan quickly becomes out of date. It is a straitjacket. We miss out on things because we stick to the plan doggedly.	

Chapter four
Leading the planning process

In a strategic planning process there can be a tendency for a few select individuals to isolate themselves from others, produce a detailed plan written in an inaccessible management-speak and then become frustrated when no-one takes the plan seriously. A better approach, which can make managing change much easier, is for an organisation to think about how a new strategy will affect the people who will be expected to implement it. Practical experience consistently shows that the sooner people who are potentially affected by change are involved in the planning process, the more likely it is that any changes will be implemented and followed through. Whatever the outcome of a strategic process, staff are more likely to work with it and feel a sense of commitment to the plan if they understand the context and what is driving it and also when they feel that they have been genuinely consulted and listened to.

However, this commitment to a democratic style of management, with an emphasis on open consultation and involvement, can have a negative side. The search for consensus can block or derail progress and can lead to a situation where change moves at the pace of the slowest. Meetings become longer, difficult decisions are avoided, the process gets delayed and innovation is strangled. In short, the greater the number of people involved, the harder it is to manage the process.

A lot depends on organisational culture and style. In some organisations, staff have deep-rooted expectations that they should be fully involved in decision-making and that everything is up for discussion. One manager observed, 'if our office caught fire the expectation would be that I would call a staff meeting to discuss how people felt about leaving the building!'

With this in mind, a key balancing act in a strategic planning process is deciding how much to push the process onwards and ensure that it does not drag on, and the extent to which people need to be consulted and involved.

Case study: strategy by proclamation

A member of staff in a national charity recounted how her organisation goes about planning and implementing its strategic plan.

Every couple of years we get a visit from one of our senior managers to 'brief us' on the organisation's new strategic plan. The process is bizarre. They disappear into residential retreats to do 'blue-sky thinking'. Experts and consultants contribute to it. Draft plans are drawn up and debated and they emerge with the new strategy.

Senior managers are dispatched to 'talk to the frontline troops' about the new strategy. These sessions can be odd. Sometimes managers make long PowerPoint presentations that bear little relationship to the issues we are dealing with, or they imply that they are consulting and engaging with us when in reality it has all been agreed. At the end of the session they often look a bit dejected as if we haven't fully appreciated the brilliance of their strategic insight. They then scuttle off back to London. The strategy is rarely ever heard of again.

It means that staff at my level either feel patronised and undervalued or become cynical and enjoy being a spectator: watching management get it wrong again.

Manage participation in the planning process

To achieve this fine balancing act you need to manage the process effectively. You will need the input of the trustees and their approval at certain stages in the process. You should seek direct input from front-line workers and volunteers. People working in the organisation should be able to contribute and participate in the big-picture discussions about vision, mission and values, for example. (See Chapter 5 for information on how to set these big-picture foundations.)

It might also be feasible to involve people who do not directly work in the organisation. Service users, carers, supporters and even funders can bring valuable insights and prevent an organisation becoming complacent or inward-looking. In organisations where this is feasible, those who are leading the planning process should set time aside to go out and engage with stakeholders to get their views on how the organisation should develop. This can be done through individual discussions, group meetings, surveys and asking for feedback on possible options.

To help you keep momentum in leading the planning process the following actions are suggested to involve people at the right level.

Be clear about the process and people's involvement

At the start of the planning process you need to be clear about the process itself: let people know how and when decisions will be made and when there will be opportunities for involvement. Try to pick appropriate times in the organisation's calendar for consultation periods and check early on when people will be available. People need to have the time to participate in the process and should have timings in their diaries as soon as possible.

Remember that the credibility of the whole process can be easily undermined if people find out that they are being consulted on something that has already been agreed.

Manage time

The whole process of involvement, consultation and participation needs to be tightly managed. If not, the process will quickly degenerate into endless meetings and many bold ideas will be killed by unmanaged consultation. A timetable should be agreed that indicates what should be happening at each stage and when decisions will be made.

Support the process

It might be useful to involve external people to facilitate and guide the process. Consultants can play a valuable role in leading the process and providing an objective and external viewpoint. However, full responsibility for the plan must lie with the organisation.

Be clear about decision-making

The process must come to an end. This might mean having to draw a line under discussions and debate and come to a conclusion. People need to know who will make final decisions on the plan and when.

Case study: what's up for consultation?

The trustees of Westbury Foundation started their strategic planning process by being very clear about their consultation process. The chair of the trustees explained how the organisation came to this point:

The Foundation had drifted. We got involved in far too many issues. Working with young people had been the original intention but other projects working with other age groups had been added on over time. After much debate, consultation at all levels and much soul-searching, we [the trustees] made the final decision to limit the organisation's role to work with young people aged 14 to 22.

Once the consultation was over and our [the trustees'] decision was made, the leadership team made it absolutely clear that the decision to target young people was closed and not up for further discussion. This was not met with resistance, however, because we had wanted the maximum input from staff about how best to work with young people and so everyone's input had been taken into account. The leadership team and staff then developed their ideas and came up with some relevant projects that we could run.

This was an important break with the past. Often staff were 'consulted' on things that had already been decided – a sure recipe for conflict and cynicism. This time senior managers were clear what was and was not up for discussion.

Structures: compartmental thinking

To set, make and disseminate a strategy successfully, people need to be able to communicate across teams and to see the overall picture.

Organisational structure is made up of decisions about how we divide up and organise work, and how accountability and processes for decision-making and communication are managed. While structures are useful in an organisation for these purposes, they can also get in the way of good communication. Many organisations traditionally divide up work by grouping people into specialist or skill-based functions. This can lead to compartmental thinking (sometimes called 'silo thinking') where people focus on their task, but don't see the whole process. For an organisation with a strategy committed to delivering services that are linked up and tackle the whole issue, this kind of structure can prove to be a barrier to success.

Furthermore, in designing new structures, managers can over-focus on structure in an academic, detached sense – drawing new charts, changing job roles and creating new processes – and forget to question if these changes will help to support the organisation's intended strategic direction.

Case study: seeing 'a bit of the jigsaw'

A long-established worker in a health agency was heard describing to a new worker how his organisation worked:

> There are three types of people here. There are a few people at the top – they tell me that they are engaged in 'creative forward thinking'. They are the 'strategists'. They spend their time turning out policies and plans. Don't ask them about the day-to-day service or funding – they are too busy being strategic for that.

> Then there are the people who deliver the work to our clients. They have to cope with meeting client needs and whatever bright ideas the first lot of people choose to drop on them.

> The third type are the fundraisers – they have to bring in the money to keep things running and also find new funding for whatever new idea has been dreamed up.

Although cynical, this experience does illustrate the problem of silo thinking, where management can become divorced from service delivery, functions such as finance and fundraising become remote and people only see their bit of the jigsaw. Few see the whole issue.

When this happens, the internal organisation is often dominated by communication gaps and conflicts. Subcultures develop. People are more loyal to their project or function than to the whole organisation.

Seeing the whole picture

To break down barriers, and encourage people to see the whole picture and how their work fits in, you need to build a different kind of organisational culture and get people to look outside their boxes. By doing so your organisation will be better equipped at all stages of the strategic and business planning process: it will allow staff to see their work in a wider context and how their effort is meant to contribute to the broader outcome.

Compartmental thinking is a particular issue in larger organisations. When organisations become larger and more complex it can become harder to put together a strategy: it becomes a remote and paper-driven exercise that matters little to most people and adds no real value to what gets done. There are several reasons why this can happen. First, different parts of the organisation do not connect together and hence the left hand does not know what the right hand is doing. People in one unit, team or location have little knowledge of what others are doing.

Second, strategic planning becomes a top-down process. Senior managers, sometimes aided by headquarters policy and planning staff, generate policies, visions and plans for the whole organisation. These documents are then 'cascaded' down the organisational structure. There is little sense of ownership or commitment to the top-down plans from those who are expected to carry them out.

And third, people relate more to their project or team than they do to the rest of the organisation. Staff understand their project or team, so strategies and plans are drawn up for their area. Turf wars break out as managers fight to protect their autonomy. There is little coordination of effort and a lack of an overall plan.

A long-standing project worker in a large national charity described his experience:

> *Working out what we were trying to do and planning how to do it was a lot easier when we were smaller. We all knew one other. Communication in the organisation was easy as people could talk to each other. As we grew and expanded this changed. People started to think and operate in groups and became loyal to their team or project. Service delivery teams had their priorities. The fundraising unit had a very different plan. Other functions such as the admin and finance and the newly created policy team seemed to operate in a kind of splendid isolation. We became a very disunited and fragmented organisation that was trying to walk or run in several directions at once.*

While compartmental thinking is a particular issue for larger organisations, smaller ones are not immune to this problem. It is a strength of smaller organisations that their size usually makes communication easier, but this is dependent on the characters of the people in the organisation. If just one person is closed and uncommunicative, or if there is any animosity between a couple of people, it can cause a serious communication blockage.

So, whatever the size of your organisation, and whether you need to build this culture from scratch or you already have an open and communicative office, the following tips can be of help, or of interest for possible ways of shaking things up. Not all examples will apply to all types of organisation but you can pick and choose those which work or adapt those which don't.

Help everyone to see how they fit in

Try to ensure that the process answers questions such as 'so, what will this mean for me?' When writing the business plan itself, make sure that the style of the plan is straightforward and it is written in plain English. The language should be expressed in the voice of the organisation (but avoiding any internal jargon) rather than alien management-speak. In this way, the plan should speak, as it were, to everyone in the organisation rather than being flat and uninspiring. (More information on writing the business plan is given in Chapter 10.)

Build in flexibility

Encourage people to go beyond their usual role: to participate in project teams or cover for colleagues. Working flexibly can help people to see things differently and gain another perspective.

Be persistent

Avoiding compartmental thinking needs constant effort. Just because people are communicating fine now, or your organisation has made recent efforts at improving lines of communication, doesn't mean this can't change suddenly. Stay vigilant.

Work back from the service user

Encourage staff to talk to the organisation's service users. How is the service-user base changing? What are their needs and expectations? What do they really need? A refocus on the service user can sometimes help people to see the bigger picture (see Chapter 5 for more on this).

Remind people of the vision and mission

Don't assume that everyone remembers the vision. People often get so involved in the detail of *what* they are doing that they forget *why* they are doing it, and management and measurement are focused on the activity and not on the result. It is useful at the start of the planning process to remind people of the *big idea* behind the organisation – what's its purpose? What does it stand for? What is meant to be different about it compared to other similar organisations? Discussions on these issues can help to inform and remind people of the vision behind the organisation, generate or rekindle some enthusiasm and sense of purpose, and show how each individual or team's work fits into a bigger picture.

Encourage learning

Encouraging people to learn new skills and expertise can help the planning process in that it helps to encourage people to identify the options that might be open to the organisation, to make more informed choices and to avoid making untested assumptions. For the learning process to be effective and to highlight ideas and developments that can be taken forward into the plan, the people engaged in the strategic process need to be open-minded, curious and willing to be challenged. The process of recognising choices can be a very positive one as it helps people to realise that they have the responsibility and capacity to shape the organisation's future development rather than just letting things happen.

One medium-sized organisation ran what they called an 'organisational teach-in day'. The day involved staff from different parts of the organisation presenting short sessions about their work to colleagues. It showed how little people knew about the different experiences and the breadth of talent and expertise that existed in the organisation. It also provided an opportunity for people to share experiences and question how services were currently organised.

Such events, or activities like internal secondments, task groups and peer shadowing, can encourage people to think outside their usual boundaries and develop new ideas for future strategies.

Explain the context

People can be so involved in coping with the day-to-day demands of keeping services going that they fail to see that the world external to the organisation is changing and how such trends could make an impact on their work. Early on in the strategic process it can be valuable if managers take time to outline how the key trends (in areas such as technology, legislation, the broader political and economic environment and changes in the profile of the people who will use the organisation) could provide opportunities or threats for the organisation. Seeing the broader picture can encourage a strategic thinking mindset and prevent people from thinking and operating in compartmental ways.

Mix people up

Getting people to work in task groups with colleagues with whom they do not usually work can help to encourage them to see things differently. Lateral team working both inside and outside the organisation is also a good idea. Groups of staff, service users and committee members can work together to carry out specific aspects of the process such as identifying future trends or exploring possible future scenarios for the organisation.

One organisation used a task group of four staff drawn from different departments to review how the organisation marketed its services. The group came up with some valuable ideas, but the insights that people gleaned from working with different colleagues were the real gain.

Let people meet and work together

Video meetings and conferencing (using services such as Skype), email and other technological processes can make internal organisational communication faster and easier, but people still need to spend time together to encourage real discussion and open up communication. Well-planned and organised staff conferences and awaydays can bring an organisation together and help people to see how their work fits in to a broader context.

See below for examples of what to avoid when planning an awayday and how to get the best from one.

Awaydays

Getting away from the organisation, having time to think through and discuss issues can bring people together and foster open communication. Such days do require careful design. Without clear objectives, structure and follow-through they can be little more than a day off.

Ten ways to waste an awayday

1. Have one because you had one last year. It's part of the routine.
2. Start the session with awkward games that make people look stupid and lack any obvious relevance.
3. Avoid difficult or challenging issues. Keep sweeping tricky or contentious issues under the carpet in the interest of team spirit.
4. Assume that everyone knows as much as you do about the external picture. There's no need to spend time looking at the context – everyone already knows that.
5. Let people be complacent and self-congratulatory. The day is a chance for people to tell each other how brilliant they all are.
6. Let some people make set-piece contributions. Allow some people to dominate the discussion.
7. Try to get a consensus when there is not one. Avoid differences or hard choices. Come up with something so woolly that no one can object to it.
8. Agree to everything. Fail to make priorities.
9. Don't agree on outcomes.
10. Don't follow through. The action and implementation will happen by itself.

Ten ways to organise an effective planning awayday

1. It's not a day off. Make sure people know that they are going to be expected to contribute, work hard and challenge assumptions.
2. Consider getting external help. A skilled facilitator or consultant, properly briefed, should be able to ensure that the day is participative, organised and productive.
3. Prepare people. Tell people what the aims of the day are before they attend. Ask them to think about some key issues or do some preparatory work.
4. Plan and agree outcomes. Make sure you are clear where you want to arrive by the end of the event.
5. Challenge current thinking. Encourage an atmosphere where people can constructively challenge the status quo and question why and how you do things. Let people ask the obvious questions: 'why do we . . . ?'.
6. Manage expectations. Be clear about the purpose of the day – can decisions be made or is it a place to develop ideas and proposals to be approved elsewhere?
7. Monitor who is and is not contributing. Watch out for some people dominating the discussion and others not contributing. Vary the methods so that everyone can be heard.
8. Be creative. Use different techniques and vary the pace. Encourage people to stretch their thinking.
9. If the day involves making decisions, pinpoint any issues which have not been agreed and decide how they will be resolved. At different points in the day, check what progress you have made and make sure that any conclusions are recorded and understood. Agree who is responsible for each action.
10. Follow up. Make sure that a written record setting out the conclusions and main action points has been produced and circulated to all who attended within 48 hours of the event.

Use exercises (such as those in this book)

Getting people to contribute to the strategic planning process requires some preparation. You need to be clear about the objective and purpose of each exercise and how the issues discussed can be carried forward into the planning process. The following points can be helpful to whoever is leading or facilitating any group planning session.

People need to feel safe

To create a good discussion, participants need to understand why they are doing it. They also need to feel confident that the discussion will be led properly, people will be listened to and confidentiality will be respected. The group leader needs to ensure that the group has clear rules to operate by and should watch out for conflicts becoming personal.

Feelings are important

Many of the exercises are about making subjective judgements. People often have gut feelings about why something is a strength or a weakness. Hard facts are important, but there should be space in the process for people to express opinions first and then work to a more objective position.

Often there is not one single correct answer

Understanding different perspectives is important. A treasurer might regard a project as a great success because it is fully funded, covers all of its costs and even brings in some money, whereas a field worker might regard the same project as dull, lacking in direction and failing to deliver. The important point is not getting to a single answer, but enabling both sides to see and understand the different perspectives. Once that has been achieved the organisation is more likely to be able to agree a shared strategy and plan.

Ensure that the discussion moves on

The group leader needs to help the group move through a discussion. A useful process is to get everyone to work on the exercise individually or in pairs, then to share each person's or pair's thoughts, identify points of consensus, discuss differing points, and then move on to identify options for future plans and development. The effective use of questions can guide the group from discussion to analysis to planning:

- **Discussion points:** What do we have in common? What are the different perspectives?
- **Analysis:** Which conclusions can we draw? Why has this happened in this way? What learning points can we draw for future actions?
- **Planning:** What options are there for the future? What kind of strategy is needed? What should the first steps be to move this forward?

Make sure the exercise is followed up

The group leader has a key responsibility to ensure that the discussion is concluded and followed up. The leader might choose to record the discussion by noting points of agreement and also points of disagreement. The leader should ensure that a process is agreed as to how the points from the discussion should be fed into the business planning process, such as by presenting options for change.

For a list of the exercises in this book, see page 9.

✐ Exercise: levels of involvement

Use this table to work out how your organisation currently consults and involves people in the process, the pros and cons of the method or methods used, and whether anything needs to change.

	Managerial method	*Effect on people*	*Potential issues*
Level 1	**No consultation:** manager draws up the plan and then informs staff of it.	Clear, quick and simple. Relevant in urgent or contentious situations.	Hard to win commitment to the plan.
Level 2	**Basic consultation:** manager asks for any views from staff and then draws up the plan.	Slightly more involvement. Doesn't hold up the decision-making process unduly.	Consultation can be tokenistic. Are staff genuinely listened to?
Level 3	**Active consultation:** manager leads a series of discussions to consult staff.	Ideas and insights from staff might make the plan stronger.	Can drag on.
Level 4	**Consensus:** all parties are actively encouraged to reach an agreement.	Can create strong buy-in and ownership.	On occasions the push for consensus can gloss over and hide conflict.
Level 5	**Delegation:** work plans are delegated to individual staff or teams.	Staff are likely to deliver on objectives that they have drawn up.	Objectives must be challenging and fit with overall strategy.

How does your organisation consult currently?

What are the pros and cons of the methods you use?

What needs to change?

Exercise: consultation and decisions – how, who and when?

Use the table to consider:

- who will give final approval to the plan?
- who will need to be consulted?

Who?	What can they bring to the process?	In which issues will they be involved?	How and when will they be involved?

Chapter five
Agreeing the big picture

Vision without action is merely a dream. Action without vision just passes the time. Vision with action can change the world.

Joel A. Barker

Almost all voluntary organisations have a constitution or governing document which says something about their aims, purpose or goals. What is written in the governing document is legally what the organisation is for. This seems a logical starting point for any planning exercise. However, sometimes this is insufficient. Constitutional aims and objectives are often written in a legal or archaic language which may not be particularly comprehensible. Some constitutions are drafted to allow a broad range of possible activities within a legal structure, and some were written so long ago that they do not feel as if they have anything to do with the organisation.

What is in the governing document rarely gives focus or direction. Usually its main role is to set out the legal powers and scope of the organisation. It is necessary therefore that, in addition to knowing what is in the governing document, everyone within an organisation is clear about what the organisation is trying to achieve and why it exists; i.e. the vision and mission must be defined and known by all. This knowledge, helped by actions and behaviour that reflect the organisation's shared values, can then provide the foundation and direction for all strategic planning.

The difference between vision and mission

The terms vision and mission often get confused or become interchangeable. To build on the definitions given on page 2, this table outlines some working definitions and offers some key questions and examples:

	Definition	Key questions	Examples
Vision	• The end point you are trying to get to. • A positive view of how your organisation wants the future to look. • Your collective aspirations.	• What will success look like? • What are you trying to change or prevent? • Who are you trying to help? • What unites and inspires you?	• 'A world without discrimination.' • 'A diverse, enjoyable, prosperous and sustainable place to live.'
Mission	• What the organisation does and who it does it for. • Creates or reinforces an overall sense of purpose.	• What's your purpose? • What do you do to meet your vision? • What is your rationale – what do you exist for? • What makes your organisation different from other similar organisations?	• To create and provide effective opportunities for young people. • To build strong and popular community organisations.

Vision

A vision provides people with a long-term view: it helps people to understand what the organisation is striving to achieve or change. It stresses the ends rather than the means and gives the organisation an overarching focus. A vision helps people to see their work in a broader context, enables them to not get bogged down in bureaucracy and processes and allows them to understand the point of each person's contribution. This in turn helps to avoid low morale and gives people a reason not to give up when things go wrong. In this way, a good vision helps to hold an organisation together and creates a feeling of unity. This can be particularly important during any periods of organisational change.

The vision should be inspiring to the people in your organisation and express a long-term outcome which can be realised one day, even if that day is far away. What would complete success look like for your organisation? The wording of your vision should be simple, memorable and punchy: a short and active sentence.

Case study: developing a shared vision

The Bowland estate had suffered years of neglect. The local council had failed to intervene to stop the estate's long-term decline. It gained a reputation for being unsafe, unpleasant and somewhere to avoid at all costs.

Anna, the worker for the estate's community forum, convened a meeting of local community groups and agencies to report that there were strong indications that the forum would be successful in winning some regeneration funding designed to build strong communities in places like Bowland. To be successful, the forum would have to submit a business plan setting out their overall vision.

The meeting started with Anna describing the main findings of a street survey of local people's concerns that she and a student on placement had carried out (see fig. 5.1).

"The estate has got such a reputation that my house is impossible to sell."
Local resident

"It's knocking our business – customers won't come in."
Local shop owner

"There's nothing to do here!"
Young person

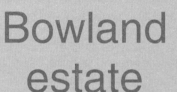

Bowland estate

"We get blamed for everything."
Young person

"No-one wants to live here."
Community activist

"The estate's a mess – I hate going out."
Local resident

"Call outs to the estate have increased 30%"
Police inspector

"I won't let my kids go to the shop alone."
Parent

"I won't go out after dark – it's not safe!"
Older person

Fig. 5.1   Street survey quotes

The discussion highlighted that the estate was in a downward cycle of decline. People were isolated, not involved and lacked any sense of optimism or pride in the estate. As one worker put it 'the only vision is getting off the estate'.

The nature of the discussion changed tone when Anna mentioned that there might be funding available. People started making suggestions for their project or their pet idea, but many of them had been tried before and had not led to much real change. This was because many of the things that groups had done in the past had been short-term and isolated from other initiatives and hence had not lasted.

Anna and the meeting's chair managed to pull the discussion back. What was needed was some sort of vision for the estate that would unite people and connect all the different activities and projects into something big.

The discussion identified three main clusters of issues:

- people feeling isolated and unsafe;
- a lack of opportunities;
- a lack of community identity and pride.

The discussion then moved on to how to develop a positive vision of Bowland in three to five years' time. They developed a vision statement: 'A safe and strong community where people choose to live and work'.

The group then met again to develop a strategy and a plan to move towards the vision and develop projects that would fit with it.

Anna commented:

> Three things were interesting: first, it would have been easy to have just focused on the funding and produced lots of isolated projects that did not add up to anything. Second, trying to develop a positive future vision of what we want to achieve really motivated and enthused people – often all we do is talk about the problems we confront and never really look at what we want to achieve. And third, the vision statement is useful in explaining and reminding us of what we are trying to do and also giving us something to measure success by.

How to create a vision

It is important to ensure that the organisation has a vision that is relevant, supported and understood. This is useful during a period of significant change in or outside the organisation or at the start of a planning process.

While the board and leadership team are ultimately responsible for the vision, time should be taken to consult staff, volunteers, service users and any other stakeholders. To get people to think about vision it can be helpful to create the space and time for them to stop focusing on day-to-day tasks and to look at some bigger and more fundamental questions. It is also important to encourage and allow them to be ambitious and confident and not to be too constrained by how things are now or by resource or funding issues. See Chapter 4 for advice and ideas on consultation.

The following five questions are useful prompts to get people working on the issue:

1. What does your latest vision state?

One starting point is to look at what is set out in the governing document. It is interesting to reflect on what it was that inspired the people who set the organisation up. If the wording in the governing document is less than inspiring there may be other sources of knowledge about why the organisation was originally set up. Another is the latest statement: is it still relevant and desirable? Does it need tweaking or updating or a more radical change? If you were starting the organisation today would you produce the same statement?

2. For whom or what does your organisation exist?

Whose interests are we working for or representing? Who do we put first?

3. What do your users want?

What are the aspirations and ambitions of the individuals and communities for whom you work? What do they want from your organisation? How do they see the vision?

4. What would success look like?

At a point in the future how will you know that you have been successful? What would success look and feel like? At what point would our work be done? How will we know that our efforts have been successful?

5. What outcomes are we interested in achieving?

What outcomes should we be focused on? What do we want to change, prevent or make different? (See below for more on outcomes.)

The answers and contributions to these questions should be recorded and reviewed. It is useful for one or two people to be in charge of editing the comments into a draft vision statement. In doing so, it is important to capture the spirit and feel of the discussions, to use plain English and to strike a balance between being realistic and achievable and a statement that is bold and demanding. A good tactic is to test that draft on people who know or use the organisation. Does the draft vision reflect their view of the organisation?

Once agreed, people in leadership roles in the organisation need to take responsibility for reminding everyone about the vision, communicating it and connecting people to it. In practical terms, this can include:

- using the vision in the organisation's publicity, branding and marketing;
- checking that all of the organisation's activities and projects can be seen as contributing to or taking the organisation towards the vision;
- reminding people of the vision when formulating plans, budgets and new projects so that they can check if proposed new ventures fit with the vision;
- using real examples and case studies to show how the organisation is inching closer to realising its vision;
- communicating the vision to new staff, volunteers, partners and other stakeholders so that the focus is on 'why we do what we do' not just 'what we do'.

Outputs and outcomes

Over the years there has been increasing interest in the terms outputs and outcomes. Policymakers and funders talk of taking an 'outcomes-based approach', i.e. focusing on the difference that your organisation can make rather than just the activities and resources. Outcomes derive from your vision, and the realisation of outcomes represents achievements along the way to achieving that vision. This section will elaborate on the definitions of outputs and outcomes that were outlined in Chapter 1, and explain why an outcomes-based approach is useful.

Definitions

Inputs, outputs and outcomes are traditionally shown as a top–down process, as illustrated in figure 5.2.

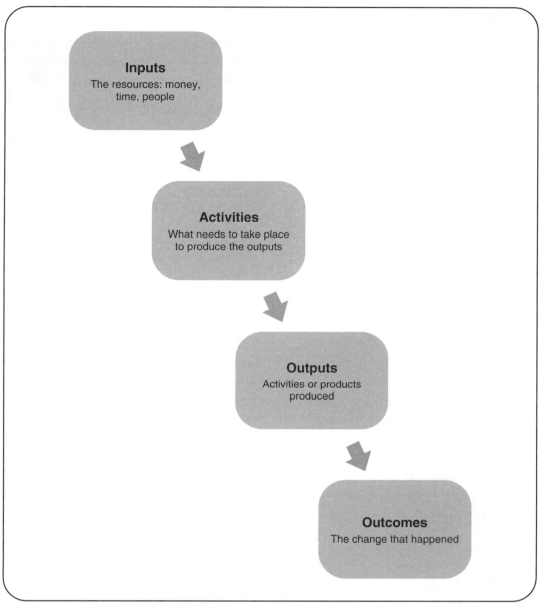

Fig. 5.2 From inputs to outcomes

Inputs are the resources and effort used in the activity. Activities in this sense are simply what needs to take place – the processes and actions – to produce the outputs. Outputs are what the organisation has produced or delivered, such as 55 advice sessions, 12 training programmes or 88 emergency accommodation places. Outcomes are the difference that you have made; some outcomes are about having created a change and others are about having prevented something negative from happening. Examples include:

- 'People able to continue to live independently.'
- 'A self-help group established and capable of running its own affairs and sustaining itself.'
- 'Young people less likely to get involved in crime.'

Focusing on outcomes

Most organisational systems such as job titles, job descriptions and structures are geared around the outputs rather than the outcomes. Giving advice, providing a day centre and running a training centre are descriptions of outputs and not outcomes. It is important to shift the focus to outcomes rather than outputs as it encourages people to pay attention to medium- to longer-term results rather than how many outputs are produced. Indeed, we often focus so much effort on managing the output that we overlook what we're aiming for. In this way, the energy required to keep delivering outputs can start to obscure the intended outcomes.

However well-managed, delivering outputs that do not work towards achieving the outcomes is pointless. As management writer, Peter F. Drucker, is widely quoted as saying, 'There is nothing so useless as doing efficiently that which should not be done at all.'

With these points in mind, setting up activities or products and therefore producing outputs without referring to the intended outcomes is not a productive or sensible use of time and limited resources. It is therefore useful to start by defining the outcomes that you want to achieve or influence and then work back to the outputs.

A helpful way to look at this is to turn the traditional inputs to outcomes diagram on its head, as shown in figure 5.3. Rather than starting with the resources needed, then deciding what needs to be done with them in the hope that they will lead to some kind of outcome, start by agreeing the short- and longer-term outcomes you want to bring about.

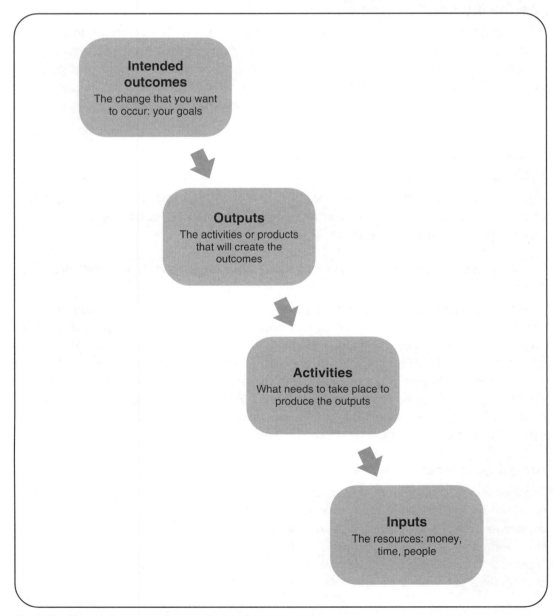

Fig. 5.3 From intended outcomes to inputs

Outcomes are hard to identify, often outside an organisation's direct control and may not be realised for some considerable time, but they are really what an organisation was set up to achieve. Outcomes come to pass when lasting change has been achieved and a difference has been made. Achieving outcomes, therefore, will take time and cannot be realised by quick fixes. Taking the outcome to input approach can highlight the following questions about the organisation's existing methods:

- Are the outputs that we currently deliver the best or most effective way of creating the intended outcomes?
- Are there any activities or outputs we manage that don't bring about the intended outcomes?
- How long has it taken us to create an outcome?
- What do we need to do to keep, support or sustain the outcome?

Answering these questions can also help people to reflect on reviewing outcomes and to set revised or new ones.

Once the outcomes have been set it is useful to consider the following questions:

Are the intended outcomes clear?

Put in another way, 'intended outcomes' are simply goals. Before you have achieved an outcome it is a goal, and after you've achieved the goal, it's an outcome. The main thing is to make sure that it is obvious what people should be aiming for so that they don't become sidetracked by inappropriate activities. Once the outcomes are clear, then you can work out what you need to do and which resources are needed to achieve your desired outcomes.

Is there a shared agreement about the outcomes?

Conflicts and tensions can sometimes occur if people have different views or expectations about what the outcomes should be. Ideally, service users, funders and your organisation should have a similar view of the intended outcomes or at least a recognition of overlapping outcomes.

How do we measure outcomes? How will we know if we achieve the outcome?

Outputs are usually easy to count, quantify and record and are mostly straightforward and unambiguous. Outcomes are often harder to quantify. The measurement of an outcome frequently requires making judgements rather than having a simple tick-box approach. This type of outcome may be difficult to measure, particularly if you're trying to show something that was prevented from happening or an altered state of being; for example, young people not becoming involved in crime, or feeling less lonely or having more confidence. Nevertheless, try to think creatively about the ways your organisation can demonstrate its impact.

Are all outcomes expected?

Some of the most significant outcomes can be the product of side-effects or things that were not in a plan. A community computer training course may have been set up originally to help older people to enjoy the advantages of computers and the Internet. However, a side-effect of reduced isolation and loneliness in that community is recorded. This may not have been planned or anticipated at the start, but these types of outcome are still worthwhile and should be recorded.

Case study: catering or care?

The Millhead charity provides meals on wheels for isolated elderly people living alone. The charity had expanded rapidly over the past few years and had appointed a coordinator to lead a dedicated team of staff and volunteers. The coordinator was soon involved in negotiating contracts with social services and producing the never-ending documentation that the social services department demanded.

A year into the post, the coordinator organised a review day with staff, trustees and volunteers. This looked at the new quality assurance standards developed at the instigation of social services. They set out various minimum standards about menu choice, food nutrition and catering management. Somehow, however, this did not feel right.

At the end of the session it suddenly occurred to the coordinator that the activity of cooking and delivering food had taken over from the charity's original purpose, to support, care for and befriend isolated elderly people. The outputs had become the priority rather than the outcomes. The means had become the end.

When the coordinator explained her feelings to the group, this brought to light others' observations. A volunteer explained that what was important to the older people to whom she was delivering meals was knowing that the same person would visit them every Tuesday and Thursday lunchtime and not how often the menu changed or how healthy the meal was. Another volunteer talked about how for some older people the actual meal was pretty irrelevant; what was important was the five minutes of conversation with the volunteer.

After the session, the coordinator worked on a plan that stressed that what the charity valued was personal care and time with elderly people. She set out some outcomes, including 'Elderly people in our community feeling connected to others'. These could then be realised in several ways such as home visiting, good neighbour schemes or helping relatives to visit more often as well as delivering food.

The mission statement shifted the focus from providing a catering service to a service providing individual care and contact delivered through a variety of activities.

Mission

Mission statements have become increasingly popular as management tools, perhaps initiated by probably the best-known mission statement, that of the USS Enterprise in *Star Trek*: 'To boldly go . . .' Many organisations have invested time in an attempt to produce similarly catchy expressions of their purpose. The process, however, can generate a degree of cynicism, particularly in instances where the statement is often little more than a vague slogan.

> *Did it really take a three-hour evening meeting and twenty flip chart sheets to produce a statement that our children's centre exists 'to be child-centred'?*
>
> Volunteer

There is a strong argument, however, for ensuring that all the people in an organisation have the same sense of purpose. After all, that is what a mission is: an organisation's *purpose*. Indeed, many organisations use the term 'purpose' rather than 'mission'. Work spent on defining the mission can help to make clear to both insiders and outsiders what the organisation is and isn't about. In this way, it clarifies the boundaries and limits of the organisation and hence helps prevent the organisation from taking on activities that take it beyond its remit and role.

The mission should also make the organisation's particular distinctive characteristics clear. Lots of agencies work with the same client group: the mission is your organisation's opportunity to show how it is different from the others.

Overall, a good mission creates a core sense of purpose from which strategy and action can follow.

Discussion about the mission can cause tension and conflict. It is not unusual to find different people in the organisation having very different ideas about what is important and what the organisation's priorities should be. Does a community advice centre exist to inform people of their rights? To encourage self-help? To campaign for social change? Or to counsel people with problems? It may well be possible to do all of these things successfully for a period of time, but when it comes to making decisions about future priorities, targets or direction, it is important to have a common view of the organisation's purpose and priorities. If the organisation tries to do everything, it could well end up fragmented and overstretched.

Indeed, without a common view of the organisation's priorities, it can experience what has been dubbed as 'mission creep' or 'mission drift'. This gives a name to the issue noted at various points in this book where, as a result of chasing funding or not keeping an eye on its core purpose, an organisation takes on too many things, dabbles in areas of work beyond its original brief and finds itself drifting beyond its core purpose and role. New and different forms of work creep in and it loses its identity and expertise.

Three activities are useful for discussing and arriving at a common view:

- identifying what drives the organisation;
- identifying what is (or should be) unique about the organisation;
- describing the organisation's work in terms of outcomes rather than outputs.

Case study: avoiding mission drift

The Dalston Carers Project was established with the specific aim of providing support to people who cared for a family member or neighbour at home. Its focus is on the carer rather than the person being cared for. The project developed a package of support services for carers to enable them to carry on caring.

The project was very effective, well-used and popular. The council's social services department was so impressed with its quality-assurance procedures and its overall management that it approached the project leader to sound her out about taking over the management of an elderly people's day centre and a volunteer home visiting scheme.

She explained the management committee's dilemma:

Our constitutional objectives are sufficiently vague to have allowed us to take on these services. It was also flattering to be asked. However, we felt that both of these activities, although needed, would have taken us away from our core business of supporting carers and changed us into being another social care agency. We politely declined.

What drives your organisation?

Voluntary organisations are driven by other motivations than simply making money. Indeed, there are usually various things galvanising a voluntary organisation at the same time.

Figure 5.4 shows four possible driving forces (but you may of course be able to think of others that apply to your organisation). All four of the driving forces will at some stages play a role in shaping the nature of your organisation. Being more motivated by any one driving force can create some organisational imbalances, as outlined in the following descriptions.

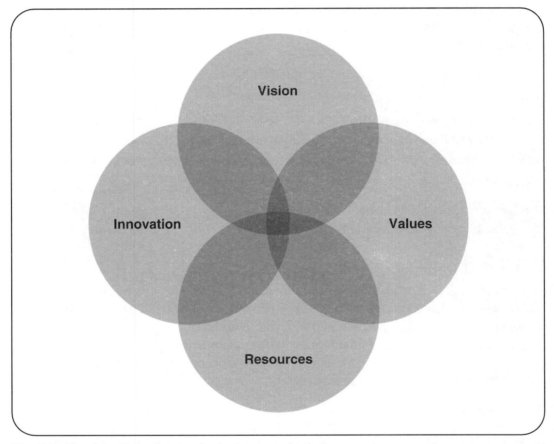

Fig. 5.4 Possible driving forces of voluntary organisations

Vision-driven

People in a vision-driven organisation feel a strong sense of commitment and purpose. An organisation that is purely or primarily driven by its vision, however, is at risk of not paying attention to the practical aspects of achieving that vision. Without sufficiently considering a strategy to direct the organisation, the right activities to carry out and hence the correct way to use its resources, it can drift in inappropriate ways. New voluntary organisations may be at particular risk of this, given that in an organisation's early days the vision will most likely be very strong but its processes weak.

Values-driven

A values-driven organisation will be strongly focused on its service users and their needs. This sort of organisation would run the risk of helping its service users to the detriment of its own existence. For example, it may offer services it cannot afford at little or no cost.

Resource-driven

A resource-driven organisation is motivated by funding and staffing its activities. Owing to its need to attract more and more resources, it can be tempted to take on inappropriate funding and projects. It can expand and do more and more, yet not become any more effective at achieving its mission and vision.

Innovation-driven

An innovation-driven organisation is galvanised by its capacity to innovate, take risks and be creative. Many voluntary organisations come into existence to do things that a public sector agency or private company would regard as not sensible practice or too dangerous to invest funds in. Innovative organisations can be exciting, dynamic and fun, but they risk being chaotic and crisis-driven and place considerable stress on individuals.

In light of these possible driving forces, consider the following questions:

- What currently drives your organisation?
- Which of these factors do you think apply most to your organisation?
- How many of these elements do you manage to combine?
- Do you already fall into any of the traps listed or are you at risk of doing so?
- Which of these motivations do you need to concentrate on developing?

The aim is to create an overall balance in the organisation so that the pitfalls of being too driven by any given motivation may be avoided.

What is unique about the organisation?

In a commercial organisation a common marketing technique is to identify a product's unique selling proposition or USP. In simple commercial terms it is what makes one washing powder different from another. The difference can be a tangible one (it performs better) or a matter of perception ('it feels right for me'). Some businesses have formed their mission statement around the characteristics and factors that make them distinct from other competitors in their market.

It is an interesting exercise to pose the question 'what is unique about our us/our service/our campaign?' and to try to list the factors that make the organisation distinctive. What would happen if the services were discontinued or the organisation ceased to exist? Would any alternatives be available? Would our service users be better or worse off? Would the organisation have to be reinvented?

Considering these sorts of questions about an organisation's uniqueness can help it to develop a strong sense of identity that holds it together internally and clarifies its purpose externally.

Case study: a muddled mission

The director of a regional museum did not expect much discussion when he tabled his draft mission statement at the quarterly trustees' meeting. The trustees were mainly academics or amateur historians who had little time for management ideas.

The draft described the mission as:

> To be a lively, open and popular educational experience. To display our collection in a creative and exciting way. To ensure that the museum is open and accessible to local people.

The chair of the trustees expressed concern that there was no mention of scholarly pursuits or of preserving the museum's collection for common heritage. One trustee said that the mission statement would be more suited to a theme park rather than a centre for study and historical research.

The director reflected on previous trustees' meetings. There had been some criticism of his proposal to recruit a marketing officer rather than fill a vacant curator's post. Another disagreement was over spending money on a schools' education pack rather than on extending the collection. The trustees showed no interest in his performance measures which showed a steady rise in visitors, they only seemed concerned with the academic credentials of the staff and the quality of the collection.

At the end of the meeting, the director agreed to redraft the mission statement in the light of the discussion. No doubt he would be able to come up with a compromise set of words that would meet his desire to have a lively and popular museum and the trustees' concern for academic excellence.

Three questions worried him, however. Would the amended wording work in practice or was he just avoiding a fundamental difference which should be resolved in a more substantial way? Was it possible to set a direction for an organisation where people were being asked to face in different directions? Could the two approaches be brought together or would the conflict escalate and lead to confusion?

By confronting these questions and the issues raised by the trustees, he realised that the two approaches were, in part, two sides of the same coin. The organisation could not offer a good educational experience without having a high-quality collection and staff with excellent credentials, and he agreed that this should be expressed in the mission. On the other hand, the museum's existence for public benefit required it to have an outward-facing aspect and so the trustees' narrow vision of the organisation needed to expand.

The director revised the mission to read:

> To be a lively and popular educational experience that is open and accessible to local people. To promote our collection's academic excellence and ensure its future.

He also proposed that the board recruit a new trustee from a more entrepreneurial background to help broaden the board's perspective and allow the trustees to challenge and support the leadership team more effectively. He communicated the importance of having a variety of people who value different aspects of the organisation and hold diverse views.

While these changes didn't remove the internal tensions entirely, they demonstrated that the criticism had been taken on board and used to improve both the mission and the diversity of the board.

Drawing up a mission statement

After becoming informed by work on what drives the organisation and what makes it unique, you should be able to produce a short mission statement for your organisation that sets out its purpose.

Good mission statements:

- are short – certainly no more than forty words;
- are focused on the value to service users and the relationship with them;
- set out the overarching goal of the organisation;
- describe the values that will influence how that goal will be achieved.

Mission statements do not need to be measurable, specific or targeted. As such, a mission statement by itself is useless. Once agreed, it must be followed up by a clear strategy for the organisation and focused objectives for its work.

Values

Values are important to a voluntary organisation. Values are:

- the ethos that underpins the organisation's purpose and work;
- the core beliefs that should influence and inform all behaviour and activities;
- what the organisation stands for.

Good values can give those in an organisation some clarity about how to act and behave and also communicate to people what to expect from the organisation. Values are the core principles and beliefs that should guide how your organisation operates and treats people. At a practical level, values should directly influence how people in the organisation behave and the decisions that get made.

Agreeing and setting out what an organisation's values are can help to develop a strong sense of unity and purpose, build and maintain teamwork and help the organisation to be successful. By doing all of this, they can help an organisation to develop a distinctive edge.

Values can be problematic, however. They can end up being just a list of random words such as 'respect', 'equality', 'fairness' and then simply displayed on a poster in the organisation's reception area. If expressed in this way, there is a danger of values merely being slogans that people take little notice of. A key task after agreeing the values is to help people see their practical relevance. Managers need to be able to explain how a value such as 'we will be open and approachable' might be carried through into how the organisation designs projects, how it markets and brands itself and how it organises its resources. Values should be regularly referred to in planning and evaluation work, in staff training and recruitment and in helping to shape the organisation's management style and culture. It requires this sort of committed approach and sustained management to turn single words or short statements into ideas that mean something for everyone in the organisation.

In some instances values can be taken too far or produce a negative result. For example, a commitment to participation and consultation in one organisation might manifest itself in endless meetings and an inability to make a clear and fast decision in another.

For values statements to mean anything they must lead to positive changes in organisational and individual behaviour. Here are some more values statements written in an active form:

- We will take responsibility for our performance in all of our decisions and actions.
- We will treat people equally and oppose discrimination in all circumstances.
- We will place the individual service user at the centre of all we do.
- We will do what we say we will do.

The director of an agency working with people with disabilities explained how having an agreed set of values gave her organisation an edge: 'there are something like 20 groups locally working on disability issues. It is the application of our values – of service user involvement, participation and respect – that gives us our identity and differentiates us from other groups.' Values can also help guide an organisation's future development. New directions, opportunities and ideas should all fit with the organisation's value base.

What roles does your organisation play?

Once the vision, mission and values are agreed and the resultant outcomes have been set, it is useful to look at what roles the organisation can play to help it on its way to achieving its vision. Organisations often take on or assume roles, and as the organisations develop, the number of roles they play can grow.

Typical roles include:

- **Advocate:** working on behalf of people to influence decisions and policies positively.
- **Campaigner:** raising public awareness to win support and achieve change.
- **Expert:** being the recognised specialist body.
- **Innovator:** finding new and effective ways of delivering services.
- **Information provider:** producing and communicating information to the public at large and specific audiences.
- **Network organiser:** coordinating, supporting and leading individuals and agencies.
- **Service provider:** managing and delivering direct services to beneficiaries.
- **Organiser/facilitator:** setting up and organising support for people with a common interest.
- **Educator and trainer:** offering programmes to develop skills.
- **Research and policy role:** monitoring and responding to new policies and practices.

Case study: role overload

The On Your Street Agency was set up ten years ago to bring some much-needed coordination and support to the ever-increasing numbers of soup kitchens, homelessness projects, detached projects and housing providers working on the issue of homelessness and rough sleeping in a northern city.

At first the organisation played a very limited role in encouraging projects to work together: it encouraged joint work and provided some joint staff-training programmes. It quickly developed a reputation for being well-managed, quick to respond and able to influence policy-makers and funders.

Three years ago, Ben, the recently appointed manager, set out on an ambitious and far-reaching plan for the organisation. As well as it continuing to provide support and training to its member organisations, three main changes happened:

1. The organisation was successful in winning a major funding programme to help fund some of the smaller projects. Its role was to act as the managing body for the fund. Projects then had to bid to it for funds and submit regular reports on what they had done.

2. The local authority asked the organisation to take over the direct management of a young persons' housing project which, due to internal problems, had experienced some major performance difficulties. Under its management, the organisation successfully turned round the project and the local authority asked it to continue to run the project directly. The organisation agreed to do this.

3. As manager, Ben became heavily involved in contributing to local policy formulation and sitting on various inter-agency partnership boards. He also developed a profile in the local media and became keen to represent the organisation and its members in the media. Ben sees his role as being to challenge existing practice and to champion the needs of the service user.

At a recent board meeting it was obvious that there was growing disquiet and concern about the organisation's direction. One of the members who managed a smaller project said that she was now confused as to what the On Your Street Agency was for: 'Is it our 'funder', is it a campaigner or is it a supporter?' Another expressed deep concern about the organisation moving into direct provision: 'Surely that takes it away from its original brief and could easily bring it into competition for funds with some of the members it is supposed to represent.' Ben decided to quietly drop his idea that the organisation should run a major awareness and fundraising campaign. The meeting agreed to return to these issues at a strategy day to be held a few months later.

In a hastily agreed debriefing, Ben expressed his frustration to his Chair and Vice Chair. He felt that all of the activities had been relevant, useful and well-delivered. Sally, who had chaired the organisation's management board from the start, reflected that the board had failed to be clear and deliberate in its plans about what roles the organisation was moving into. Too many things had gone through 'on the nod'. People hadn't seen a strategic pattern. Sally also felt that the organisation was in danger of taking on far too many roles and that it needed to be very careful about roles that could conflict with its core purpose to support and coordinate.

It was agreed to hold a strategy day which would need to approve which roles were relevant and which were not.

Case study: playing different roles

The Heathgrove Network identified an evolution through several roles in its 15-year history. The network was established by a group of parents whose children had a drink or drugs problem.

The network's committee identified three different phases:

Early-stage years: 1–3	Mature-stage years: 3–10	Renewal years: 11–15
When it started, the group's main role was to provide mutual aid and support to parents. In time, the group members started to act as an advocate to policy-makers.	The success of the early stages led to the group having a high profile. It started to win funding and employ staff. By year 5 the network was running an information service, providing direct services and developing new and innovative ways of working with clients. This phase led to organisational expansion and a change in the style and culture of the network.	The renewal phase came after some serious discussions about the role and purpose of the network. The management committee agreed to focus on three main roles: ● To be regarded as the lead or expert body. ● To campaign for better service provision. ● To educate and train other agencies in how best to work with families.

As Heathgrove evolved through these roles, the character and style of the organisation changed. The early stages were informal with an emphasis on mutual self-help. In the middle stage the emphasis shifted to delivering services, and the third stage was an attempt to develop the influencing and campaigning work. It was interesting to note that the movement into these roles had evolved and was never deliberately planned.

Case study: an unintended role

The Boxtree Resource Centre regularly arranged for its van, and Stan the driver, to be used by the local young people's homelessness project to move its clients into new and more stable accommodation. In terms of the centre's formal performance monitoring, the three to four bookings a month did not amount to much.

Roz, the centre's manager, had noted that these bookings took up a lot of Stan's time for the journey involved. In a casual conversation she realised that Stan was doing a lot more than simply driving the van and helping to shift people's belongings. He would help to settle the young person into their new home by showing how all the appliances worked, ensuring that they had everything they needed and explaining where local shops and other amenities were. On some occasions, he would help the young person to plan how they were going to manage their money or do a few basic DIY jobs. This help was well beyond what he was formally employed to do and he was bending the rules, but feedback from the homelessness project and the housing associations was that Stan's support was highly valued and often a crucial factor in getting the tenancy off to a good start.

Roz realised that the centre was in much more than the transport and removals business. Stan had developed a valuable service that provided crucial support at a challenging and difficult time for a young person. His service delivered outcomes that were about promoting independence and tackling homelessness. Over time, Roz and Stan developed a 'settling in service' that they offered successfully to other social landlords and homelessness projects. It extended the centre's role, created a new income stream and helped it to achieve key outcomes.

Exercise: what if we did not exist?

This is a very simple exercise to start people thinking about their organisation's vision, purpose and roles.

If we did not exist:

What would be different?

Who would miss us?

What impact would it have on the world if we did not exist?

Would we have to be reinvented?

Exercise: working out a mission statement

These questions are designed to help you draft a mission statement for your organisation.

Objectives

What are the objectives and purpose of the organisation as set out in the constitution?

Original aim

Why was the organisation set up? What was the original purpose?

Outcomes

What outcomes do you want to bring about?

Difference

What differentiates us from other similar organisations?

Review your answers, spot key words or concepts and use the information to produce a statement of no more than 30 to 40 words.

Exercise: working out your values

This exercise aims to help you establish the core values that should underpin your organisation's strategy. To get the most out of it, try keeping to the following rules:

- Use plain English and simple words.
- Avoid jargon.
- Describe the values in active terms, i.e. how you will behave.

What are the core principles that should hold your organisation together?	
How would you want to see people treated by your organisation?	
In which ways do you want your organisation to be different from others?	
What do you want your organisation to stand for?	

Set out your organisation's core values:

✎ Exercise: what roles do you play?

Role	Current involvement 1: Very high 2: High 3: Moderate 4: Low	How might this role develop in the future?	Is it likely to: ● increase ● decrease ● stay the same?
Advocate			
Campaigner			
Expert body			
Innovator			
Information provider			
Network organiser			
Service provider			
Organiser and facilitator			
Educator and trainer			
Research and policy role			
Other roles:			

How many roles is it viable to play at one time? How do these roles fit with our mission?

Chapter six
Analysis

The future ain't what it used to be.

Arthur C. Clarke, Yogi Berra and others

This chapter looks at how organisations can collect and interpret information in order to feed it into the business plan.

Three types of information are needed to inform and develop the plan.

1. Information about external developments

This information is about the changing state of the organisation's market; i.e. the level and type of demand for the organisation's services. You will need to think about:

- known factors that will demand a response;
- predicted factors/trends that could require a response, including:
  - new ways of working and developments in the sector and similar agencies;
  - new needs and types of service users;
  - the extent of need for what you do;
- comparisons with similar agencies.

2. Information about internal performance

You will need to explore:

- the stage of development of the organisation's activities and the organisation itself;
- the key strengths and weaknesses of activities and the organisation;
- ideas for developing activities and the organisation (see Chapter 7, page 110).

3. Information about the business and financial position

You should explore:

- what activities cost to operate (see Chapter 8, page 145);
- estimates of future income (see Chapter 8, page 139);
- break-even and break points (see Chapter 8, page 141).

Using a SWOT analysis to get started

A very well-established planning tool which considers both internal and external factors is SWOT (strengths, weaknesses, opportunities and threats) analysis. It is a good starting point for thinking about analysing your organisation.

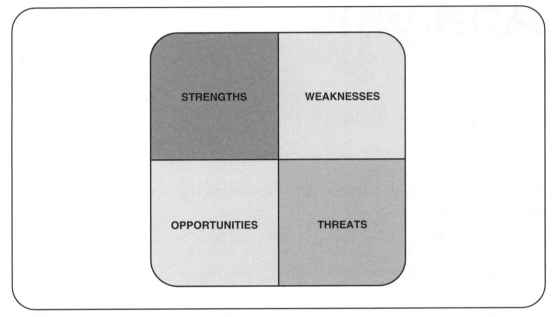

Fig. 6.1   SWOT analysis

In a SWOT exercise participants contribute their assessment of the organisation in terms of its strengths and its weaknesses, and their ideas about its future: the opportunities and threats (as shown in fig. 6.1). People tend to find it easier to identify weaknesses and threats rather than strengths and opportunities. It is often useful, therefore, to insist that participants identify a minimum number of strengths and to keep the following points in mind:

● What some people see as a weakness others may see as a strength. One person might see a day centre as being disorganised and unprofessional. Another might see it as relaxed, friendly and accessible to the intended client group. Discussion about such different perceptions can be really valuable.

● Often things are neither an opportunity nor a threat – they occupy the space in between. A new funding regime, for example, could go either way.

● Discussion time is often focused on overcoming the weaknesses. However, it is worthwhile to spend time on the strengths and to focus on which factors created their success.

SWOT analysis is a good way of capturing the issues facing an organisation and eliciting the different views of a range of people.

Taking the SWOT further

Once the four elements of SWOT have been completed it is useful to spot key issues and themes. Discussion needs to move on beyond analysis and look at what actions are needed.

A simple way of doing this is to look at each subject box and ask:

● **Strengths:** which actions do we need to take to consolidate and keep them?

● **Weaknesses:** which actions are needed to overcome them? Could any of the weaknesses be turned around and become an opportunity?

- **Opportunities:** do they need some further work or investment?
- **Threats (often organisational risks):** what action is needed to protect the organisation against them?

Thinking about moving from analysis to action is a useful way of getting people to identify future strategy and actions.

Predicting change

An important part of the strategic planning process is being able to predict, or at least cope with, change. With this in mind, another useful starting point in the analysis stage is to identify the different kinds of change that your organisation is experiencing or is about to experience both internally and externally. Here are four types:

Type:	Imposed changes...	External changes...	Proactive changes...	Organisational and cultural changes...
	• Often have a level of urgency and potential crisis about them. They are usually outside your control, but you have to respond to them. Failure to act swiftly and decisively could put you or your organisation in jeopardy.	• Are about things that are happening or are likely to happen outside the organisation and include developments, trends and factors in your external environment. They could be positive or negative, opportunities or threats or a combination of both. • Some are easy to identify whereas others are more emerging trends.	• Are those that you decide to make, are more in your control and are more strategic. They are usually about how you (or the people leading the organisation) want your organisation to develop or be, taking the initiative and resolving to go for it.	• Are usually internal changes and are those regarding how the organisation operates. The organisation's style and individuals' personal behaviour, roles and management styles can all be factors. They are essentially changes in the way things get done.
Examples:	• A decision by a key funder to cut its funding to your organisation by 10%. • The publication of a negative inspection report about your organisation.	• Changes in the profile of the community you serve. • Forthcoming legislation.	• Your decision to prioritise work with poorer communities. • Your decision to set up a joint campaign with other agencies.	• Giving greater respect and choice to service users. • Moving to a flatter organisational structure.

Once the different changes facing the organisation have been identified it is useful to focus discussion on:

- which of the changes are really significant;
- which issues could be clustered together;

- whether there is a logical order in which you should tackle them – i.e. if one is dependent on another;
- whether you need to be proactive and strategic to avoid simply responding to other people's agendas.

The following case study shows how one organisation carried out this exercise.

Case study: predicting change

The Gollan Centre provides support, care and advocacy for older people. The centre trustees, staff and service-user representatives used this exercise at the start of their planning process to summarise which changes the centre would be likely to face and the key issues that their new strategy would have to respond to.

Imposed change	External change	Proactive change	Organisational and cultural change
- Our building is no longer fit for purpose. - The Safe at Home service is close to breaking point. - Funding for the successful advocacy project ends in six months.	- People are living longer – demand will increase. - Changes in adult social care: the council is doing and providing less. Do we pick up the pieces? - More competition: other agencies are moving in on what we do.	- Agreed that our main focus should be on rights and advocacy not direct service delivery. - We have a commitment to work with others. Who can we collaborate with? - We need some stability and more sustainable income streams.	- Aim to work *with* older people rather than work *for* them. - Want to work at a strategic level by influencing policy-makers.

Analysis

Which of the changes are really significant?	- Much harder and tougher financial position - Services are under pressure - Need to be very clear about our role
Can any issues be clustered together?	- Demand for our services - Funding - Developing our strategic role
Is there a logical order in which you should tackle them; i.e. is one dependent on another?	1. Stabilise situation 2. Clarify our role and priorities 3. Develop and implement a funding plan 4. Communicate with partners
Do you need to be proactive and strategic to avoid simply responding to other people's agenda?	- Develop a new funding plan - Be proactive with partners – explain our role - Be clear about what we can and can't do

Two key themes emerged in the discussion that followed: first they felt that the Gollan Centre was in, or fast approaching, a perfect storm, with increased demand, greater competition and fewer resources. Second, a lot of discussion centred on what role the centre should play – should it be a direct provider of services to older people or should it mainly focus on advocacy and campaigning?

At the conclusion of the discussion the meeting posed four challenges for a newly appointed strategy task group to develop options and work on:

- If we want to focus on advocacy, campaigning and playing a strategic role, what are the implications of this? Which areas of work might we need to withdraw from? How can we fund this role?
- Do we need a different kind of business model? Can we be a sharper and smaller organisation?
- Relations with others: how do we fit with other agencies that work with older people? Do we collaborate or do we compete? What should our distinctive role be?
- Monitoring what's happening: how can we get an overview of what is happening to older people? Is it our role to feed issues back to policy-makers?

The exercise and the structured follow-up discussion helped to give a clear direction and focus to the centre's planning process.

See page 97 to try this exercise in your organisation.

External developments

In the 1960s and 1970s large corporations and public agencies invested heavily in business planning and tried to sift information, analyse issues and forecast the future. These planners produced comprehensive ten-year documents that even in more stable times became quickly outdated or were out of date the day they left the printers. The reality is that our capacity to predict the future accurately is very limited, so any attempts are likely to be not particularly accurate and probably downright wrong!

Trends

A part of good strategic management is being able to respond quickly and effectively to new developments and events. A key skill – if not an art – is being able to spot a trend, i.e. the general direction in which something is changing, early enough and being able to respond to it in a proactive rather than a reactive way. There are trends and developments in all activities that could shape an organisation's future. A better approach therefore is to identify trends, assess how they may have a potentially positive or negative impact on the organisation and work out the best ways to respond to them. Ideally, you want your organisation to be one step ahead of the game: to be well prepared for the trend and perhaps even able to turn a potential threat into an opportunity.

A failure to recognise trends can lead to an organisation missing opportunities, being pushed into reacting to things or becoming irrelevant and out of date.

Inevitably, trend-spotting involves a degree of judgement. It helps to ask yourself some questions, such as:

- How significant do you expect a trend to be?
- Which trends should you react to?
- Where should you invest your time and resources?

Five types of trends

1. **Available resources.** What might happen to the different kinds of resources your organisation needs? Examples here could include changes in funding levels and in funders' policies and priorities and the availability of staff and volunteers.

2. **Changes in practice.** What kinds of changes might there be in the way that you work? This could include new ways of delivering services, changes in technology, and new methods and work practices.

3. **Changes in demand and need.** This includes changes in the service user or community profile, demographic change and changes in what service users might want, need or expect.

4. **Changes in the political or economic arena.** This is about the potential effect of changes in the outside world. Examples include broader changes in how people are living and how society operates, political direction and new legislation.

5. **Changes in the sector/market.** This could include what other organisations are doing, potential competition or changes in the sector or market that you operate in.

Case studies: predicting trends and developments

A social care charity

Some of the key future issues for a social care charity are set out in this table.

	Next 12 months	1–3 years	Longer term
Available resources	Fundraising from the public will stand still or decline.	The lease will expire on building.	We have a long-term aim of service user control and management.
Changes in practice and how we work	Some services will be at breaking point if demand continues.	External evaluation of project is scheduled.	Our clients will get older. Families may increasingly struggle in their caring arrangements and demand for help may increase. Our service users may make greater demands for choice and independence.
Changes in demand and needs	How will local NHS and community care reforms work in practice and what effect will they have on us?	What impact will the recession have on our service users and carers?	Voluntary agencies will be increasingly likely to take over services that were previously statutory.
Changes in the political or economic arena		A possible move to a new local authority structure.	We may conflict with other providers over values.
Changes in the environment and market	Will we need to cooperate or compete with similar agencies?	Commissioners increasingly expect us to have a formal quality assurance system.	

A national health charity: examples of trends

The staff team of a national health charity which provides support to people with a long-term medical condition identified twenty key trends that could have an impact on their work and would need to be considered as part of their strategic planning process:

1. Much greater knowledge about the disease
2. More media interest
3. People will expect instant information
4. Greater use of the internet
5. Some people will not be online
6. Medical advances – new drugs
7. A lack of independent and objective information about the condition.
8. Other agencies doing what we do
9. Greater competition between charities
10. Information overload from all media dilutes the charity's message
11. Possible legislative change that could affect patients
12. Other agencies asking us for information
13. Greater public awareness of the disease
14. Local groups in our network starting to campaign
15. Tougher fundraising climate
16. New ways to fundraise
17. Some interest from parliamentarians
18. Some supporters can't/won't join local groups
19. Offers of sponsorship from drug companies
20. People wanting information outside office hours

The team decided to focus on four key issues:

- greater use of technology;
- other agencies getting involved in our work;
- medical developments – new drugs;
- more media interest.

The team felt that these four issues would be critical for the organisation and therefore would need to be high on the agenda. The team decided to look at the best ways the organisation could respond by looking at the charity's four main areas:

- the network of 30 local groups spread throughout the country;
- the campaign team;
- the information service;
- the fundraising team.

	Greater use of technology	*Other agencies getting involved in our work*	*Medical developments – new drugs*	*More media interest*
Local groups	Explore ways of networking with local groups. Some groups could meet on the Web rather than in person.	Consider potential for local collaboration. Danger of competition.	Provide regular updates for local groups.	Encourage local groups to appoint volunteer press officers. Provide training and support to volunteer press officers in order to increase local coverage.
Campaign team	Set up an e-campaign group.	Consider creating a joint agency alliance to lobby government.	Carry out research to monitor spending on drugs – is there fairness across the country?	Develop contact with specialist health journalists. Feed them positive stories and ideas for features.
Information service	Shift from paper to electronic communications. Work out how we charge for web-based information.	Benchmark our information service against others.	Produce specialist and up-to-date information on new drugs. Create special section on the website.	Evaluate whether the information service can continue to field all press calls. Do we need a full-time press officer?
Fundraising team	Ensure that people can donate online on our website.	Consider the implications for more competition in funding. Pursue a stronger brand identity.	Approach drug companies to sponsor our work or advertise in our publications. Develop an ethical policy on this.	Build further on the greater awareness which has been created.

The exercise 'Predicting trends and developments' on page 98 provides a format that can be used to record trends and to present them in the business plan itself.

Ways to identify real and future trends

- **Listen to your service user.** Current service users can be a good reference point. How are their needs and expectations changing? What thoughts do they have on how needs have changed?
- **Analyse your own data.** Most organisations collect and collate data about their performance, usually as a funding requirement. These performance measures or indicators are rarely analysed or used in any constructive way. Looking at the data and spotting changing patterns over time can highlight underlying trends.

- **Link up with your sector.** Being involved in your sector, attending conferences and participating in other network events and activities can be a valuable way of learning what others are thinking and identifying possible developments.

- **See the bigger picture.** Reading relevant journals or websites can help you to understand the context in which you are operating.

- **Look at what you don't do.** It is interesting to look for potential gaps and unmet needs. How often does your organisation turn people away because 'we don't do that'? How frequently do people use your services because, although it isn't really what they want, it is all that is available?

- **Compare and contrast.** Looking at what other similar organisations are doing can be a valuable way of spotting relevant trends (see below).

- **Build links with experts.** Developing relationships with expert practitioners, academics and researchers can be a useful way of keeping in touch with trends. Some organisations have developed advisory panels to encourage this process.

- **Encourage reflection at work.** Getting staff in supervision sessions or team meetings to reflect occasionally on how the work is changing can be a source of useful trends.

- **Talk to commissioners and funders.** Public sector commissioners are taking an increasingly strategic approach to how they commission services and many are developing better use of evidence and data to help them in the commissioning process. Commissioners and funders, therefore, often have access to data and an overview of what is happening – current trends, gaps and potential developments – that can be a valuable source of information.

After identifying trends

Once you have identified some trends it can be useful to see if any can be grouped together into relevant clusters. They can, for example, be divided into:

- **facts:** trends that we know will happen;
- **opinions:** assessments based on experience of past trends;
- **guesswork:** hunches about what might happen.

After listing and grouping the trends it is useful to:

- decide which ones are going to be key issues or drivers for the organisation;
- discuss the best ways for the organisation to respond and make it an opportunity;
- identify the first steps that should be taken to respond appropriately to any trends and create those opportunities.

Making comparisons with similar agencies

Another form of external analysis is to look at how the organisation relates to and fits with other agencies doing similar or related work. This can be useful in identifying potential conflicts or duplication of effort, but more positively to identify gaps in provision and potential for cooperation, alliances and joint work.

The first step is to list all the organisations which do (or might be perceived as doing) similar things to your organisation. Few organisations have identical comparators, so list any which do similar things to yours.

Once a list has been completed, it is useful to compare the key similarities and differences between each agency and yours and then go on to look at the relationship between agencies and how it might develop.

To analyse the relationship, focus on the following questions:

- What's different or special about what we do compared to others?
- Can we use what is unique about us to market or promote the organisation?
- If we were to map the areas of provision of each organisation, in which places do we overlap?
- What potential is there for cooperation, joint ventures, alliances and even mergers?
- Should we cooperate or compete?

It is also useful at this stage to look at how other agencies' strategies and policies might have an impact on your work. For example, if your organisation were to identify opportunities for a local children's project, it might be useful to see the local authority's children's service plan.

 Case study: looking outside

A locally managed housing advice project carried out this exercise to look at how it related to other agencies which did similar work to it. The following chart is a summary of their analysis.

Agency	Similar to us	Different from us	Relationship	Strategic issues
Citizens Advice Bureau	• Operates an open-door policy. Very busy.	• Part of a national service. • Has a strong public profile. • Uses volunteers.	• Good – we have had joint training.	• Potential for more joint work.
Law Centre	• Very busy.	• Appointments only. • More specialist.	• Lost contact due to staff changes.	• Need to re-establish contact.
Housing Aid Centre at the Town Hall	• Town centre location.	• Only does housing advice. • Directly managed by the council.	• Poor relationship in the past.	• Could we be seen as rivals? • We potentially overlap. • How can we work together?
Solicitors in private practice		• They are profit-making. • Expensive. • Sometimes act for landlords.	• Mixed – some good personal relationships.	• Could we encourage pro bono work?

To try this exercise, see page 99.

Internal performance

The analysis part of the planning process should also be an opportunity to take a fresh look at the kind of services and activities the organisation is involved in and to assess their strengths and weaknesses. This should be a chance to renew and revitalise activities by challenging them and agreeing how they can best develop. The business plan, as chapters 9 and 10 will show, needs to demonstrate that the organisation has thought critically about its current operations and that some kind of objective appraisal of all of its activities has been done.

Understanding lifecycles

There are different stages both in the development of activities within an organisation and in the organisation itself. If you can work out where they are in their lifecycles you can better understand potential future challenges and work out what needs to be done to advance the activities and the organisation.

Stages in the development of activities

Consider where each of your organisation's activities is on the lifecycle diagram set out in figure 6.2.

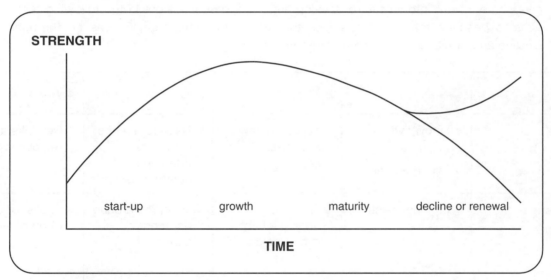

Fig. 6.2 A programme lifecycle

Start-up

The activity is new. People are still trying to establish it and build up their expertise. It is innovative and those working on it are keen to try new things. This stage involves a lot of hard work and a lot of learning.

Growth

Assuming that the start-up is successful, the activity may well grow. More activities are developed and new services are rolled out to more people. Often success in this stage leads to more opportunities and more work. The profile of the activity is usually high.

Consolidation/maturation

At this stage the activity is on a plateau. It is delivering services in a safe and reliable way. An element of routine creeps in. Systems become important.

Decline

At this stage there is little energy or innovation left. The activity is inclined simply to repeat what it has always done. Those carrying it out just go through the motions. New work is left for start-up projects. This stage can lead to a fall in quality or a crisis.

Renewal

The final stage is about renewal. This usually involves tackling the decline. The activity needs to be re-evaluated and given a fresh focus. Sometimes activity needs to be relaunched or brought to a close.

After considering at which stages of the lifecycle your organisation's activities are, it is worth reflecting on a few questions:

- How long does the cycle take for each service/activity?
- What are the critical issues at each stage?
- What sort of management style is needed at each stage?
- How do you manage decline or closure of a service/activity?

Stages in the development of organisations

Examining how your organisation has developed and trying to understand its history can give some insight into its future development. The model set out in the following table aims to describe the different stages that many voluntary organisations go through. Decline and/or closure is an alternative to renewal.

	1. Start-up	2. Growth	3. Consolidation	4. Renewal
Theme	• Innovative • Vision-led • Experimental	• Takes on new activities • Grows fast	• Delivers a range of services, often on a contract basis	• Rethinks and refocuses
Key issues	• Founder-centred	• Grows by adding lots of initiatives and projects	• Is geared around delivering services	• Looks for clarity of purpose
Style	• Informal • Entrepreneurial • Task-led • Dynamic	• Becomes focused on delivering services • Starts to get organised	• Has to demonstrate the delivery of outputs and outcomes. • Becomes more efficient and organised	• Redevelops campaigning and advocacy
Funding	• Reactive • Happy to take any available funding	• Seeks funding for specific projects • Goes for funding which is a popular choice at that time	• Seeks mixed funding: grants, contracts and fees	• Diversifies funding

Organisational issues	• Lacking in procedures and policies	• Creates plans, systems and measures. • Looks for ways to fund core costs, not just projects • Starts to become specialised in one or more areas	• Becomes just another service provider? • Management costs rise	• Creates a clearer sense of mission, purpose and independence
Management issues	• Dominated by leadership rather than management	• Looks for ways to hold it all together and to be more than a collection of projects	• Endeavours to develop management systems	• Needs to evaluate its impact

First stage: start-up

The organisation is driven by a compelling vision of what it wants to achieve or change or by a strong motivation to get things done. At this stage the organisation is often led by one or two key individuals who project the vision, hold it all together and set the tone, pace and direction. The organisation lacks procedures and processes and funding is normally sought as a means to an end. This stage is characterised by hard work, energy and creative innovation.

Second stage: growth

Movement into the second stage is often driven by successes in the first. The organisation's energy and dynamism attracts people. The organisation expands by taking on new initiatives and projects. The need to be organised (or at the very least legal) is recognised. Rules, policies and procedures are needed to ensure proper services are run and to meet contractual obligations and funders' expectations.

Third stage: consolidation

The third stage can be characterised by the organisation strengthening how it organises and manages its activities, searching for efficiency and being focused on service delivery. Systems, procedures and processes are produced. The organisation's core expands and functions and specialisms such as personnel or fundraising develop. Costs rise as levels of management and administration are added.

Fourth stage: renewal

The fourth stage is about rethinking and refocusing. The organisation needs to revisit its purpose. It may have expanded and grown away from its original vision. It is not sufficient at this stage for the organisation simply to get bigger – it needs to review all its activities to see if they really make a difference to service users.

Several things can happen as your organisation moves through these stages.

Disruption

The movement between stages is often gradual but can nevertheless be disruptive. People frequently leave between stages. Individuals who might be very effective at creating a vision, involving others and being innovative in the first stage might not be so good at creating the sound management systems and procedures needed in the later stages as the organisation grows.

A culture clash develops

As an organisation develops and grows its style, the atmosphere and informal ways of doing things change. One worker described what this was like in his organisation:

> When we started out it was all very informal, everyone mucked in. As the organisation grew, it changed. People stopped seeing the whole picture. They started being only interested in their own project or bit of the organisation. Fundraisers, admin and project staff all developed their own subcultures, which at times clashed or at best failed to communicate.

The funding model changes

The organisation's funding mix and relationship to funders change. To start the organisation, funding is often obtained from any available source. A trustee of a new organisation recalled how 'in the early days we grabbed whatever funding was going'. As the organisation develops, growth is often achieved through project funding, where the organisation wins contracts to deliver certain funds. This can mean that some parts of the organisation are well-funded while others suffer.

A key issue is to work out how to fund the organisation's administrative and managerial core. Funders pay for the organisation to *deliver* an output rather than simply *funding* it. The work involved in managing funding increases because funders want to monitor information to ensure that the organisation is delivering on its objectives. The organisation aims to develop what one manager described as a 'mixed economy' of funding – a mixture of grant aid, service or project contracts plus an element of earned income through developing forms of trading or charging for some services.

The skill basis changes

New skills are often needed in the move from one stage to another. The entrepreneurial skills needed to turn an idea into an organisation, win funding support and inspire others to be involved are different from the organisational management skills needed in the second and third stages. In these stages the emphasis is on implementing systems, planning, controlling resources and ensuring that the organisation is legally compliant, has proper policies and procedures and can deliver a consistent service.

The key strengths and weaknesses of activities

Case study: comparing resources and results

The Meadows Charity

The Meadows Charity provides a range of services and activities for a diverse population over six small to medium-sized rural towns. At the time of the review it had four main goals:

- To support and encourage volunteering
- To support young carers
- To encourage community involvement and new opportunities
- To build strong communities.

A sub-group of trustees and staff produced some analysis of current projects and activities in order to compare the resources used with the outputs produced. The level of success of each project or activity was also evaluated from low to high.

Comparing resources and outputs

Stage 1: list the organisation's main activities and projects	Stage 2: assess outputs for each activity or project over the past few years and consider level of success	Stage 3: list the inputs used to deliver each activity
Volunteer campaign	• High: 60 people identified as volunteering. • Development worker spent two days per week supporting and training volunteers	• Development worker: three days a week. • Administration assistant – two days a week. • We have a £9,000 budget.
Running four community shops	• Low to medium: three shops struggling to break even and stay open. One shop is having moderate success.	• Volunteer time: 50 hours each week. • Two to three days of staff time to support/cover shops.
Managing the Meadows Community Festival	• Medium to high. • 900 people attended: down slightly from previous years. • 100 local volunteers involved in the festival.	• Takes over the whole organisation in the weeks leading up to the festival. • Costs increasing. • Festival budget: £15,000.
Young carers' support group	• High: successful work with 17 young carers. • Strong support from schools, health agencies and others.	• Four days a week, full-time worker. • Significant support from our manager and other staff.
Community gardens	• Medium: three gardens and allotments now operating involving 16 local people.	• Development worker: two days a week.
Summer play scheme	• Low to medium: operates for six weeks. • Participation numbers declining.	• High cost due to staffing ratios. • A lot of staff time.
Four internet cafés/ computer skill classes	• High: very popular. Successful collaboration with local college.	• We facilitate it but don't directly deliver it. Takes about a day of our time.

All of the activities can then be plotted on axes as shown in figure 6.3 to compare the resources used with the outputs delivered.

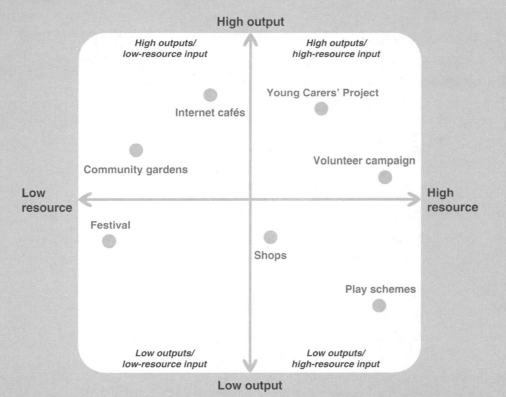

Fig. 6.3 Resources versus outputs

In their post-exercise discussion the following points were recorded to take forward into the business planning process:

Analysis: how does our use of inputs compare with our outputs? Are there any activities that take up lots of resources, but deliver no or hardly any outputs? Are there any outputs that we delivered which did not involve many inputs?

- Our internet cafés and community gardens are good value: they deliver a high number of outputs with a low level of resources used.

- Our Young Carers' Project and volunteer campaign use a lot of inputs but are worth the resources needed.

- Our festival doesn't cost us much resource-wise but isn't delivering enough towards our outcomes.

- Our shops and play schemes are a drain on the organisation.

Plan ahead: ideas and issues for future strategies

- Should we continue with the shops and the play schemes? Can we reduce the level of resources used and/or increase the number of outputs? What impact would our withdrawal have on the charity?

- How do we stop the festival from declining and taking up more resources for fewer outputs? Are we prepared to invest more in it to stop it declining?

- How can we do more work that is as successful as our internet cafés? Could they be the basis of a future business model where we facilitate other agencies' involvement and share the cost?

To try this exercise in your organisation, see page 100.

Portfolio analysis

Another way of evaluating an organisation's outputs is to consider using one of the established tools used in the commercial world. The Boston Consulting Group developed a useful business tool for companies, known as the Boston matrix, to enable them to analyse their various products and services as a portfolio. With a little adaptation it can be applied to voluntary organisations that offer several projects and services. The matrix is formed as shown in figure 6.4.

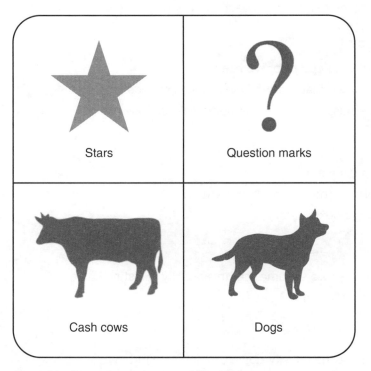

Stars

Question marks

Cash cows

Dogs

Fig. 6.4 Boston Consulting Group's product portfolio matrix

Question marks are projects and activities that are still being developed but have the potential to become stars. They take up resources, but as yet are not fully delivering. Question marks could be a start-up project, a pilot activity or even an idea that is being developed.

Stars are currently particularly strong and may have potential for growth. They are dynamic, popular and creative. Some stars are short-lived shooting stars.

Cash cows are reliable and mature services and activities. They operate well and often provide a degree of stability in the organisation. There is a danger of cash cows being ignored or taken for granted.

Dogs take up time and resources, but produce little of value in return.

Several strategic options can be identified from working through this model.

- What criteria are being used? In a profit-making venture the criterion is usually a simple one of 'how high is our market share?' or 'is it bringing in a profit?' You will need to agree which criteria are important to your organisation, such as: Does it work towards our goals or deliver outcomes? Is it what our service users want?

- What should the balance be? How does your organisation balance being risky and innovative (by having stars and question marks) and the need for stability (by having cash cows)? How do you get a balanced portfolio? How much time should you put into developing new ideas into projects that will replace the dogs?
- How do activities move through the matrix? Today's dogs might well have been last year's stars. Are you really evaluating and planning your work? What are the factors that make things work?

Strategic questions to ask about each activity placed in each box are:

Question marks

- How long does it need to prove itself?
- How will we know that it is working and is a success?
- How prepared are we to manage some risk and failure?

Stars

- What makes it a star?
- Can we replicate these factors elsewhere?
- Where will it go next?

Cash cows

- For how long can we assume that this activity will stay stable?
- Do we take it for granted?

Dogs

- Should we close the activity down or reinvest effort in it?
- Why has it been left in this box?
- What options do we have?

The aim is to make the portfolio balanced with a mixture of stars, cash cows and question marks, where the cash cows provide the funds for the future growth of question marks which become stars.

Case study: Youth Development Agency's portfolio analysis

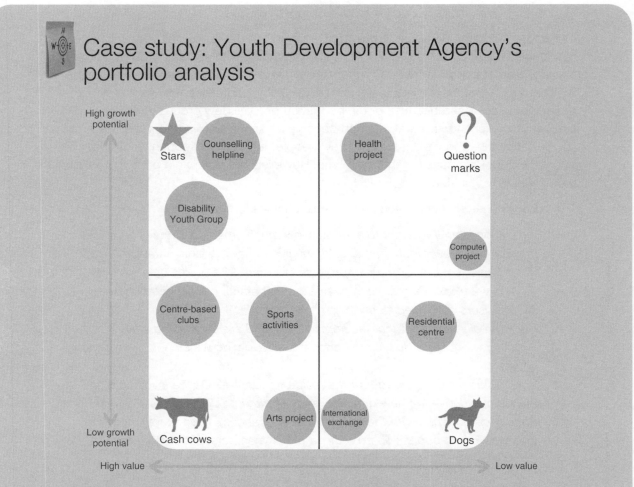

Fig. 6.5 Youth Development Agency – product portfolio matrix

The **question mark** quadrant contained two new projects. First, a health project that was still very much at a pilot stage. No-one knew if it would work, but it was considered worth investing in. Second, the computer project. This project had been around the organisation for two years. It had attracted little interest from service users (or funders) and really was little more than the pipe dream of a particular worker.

The **stars** quadrant consisted of two new projects that were breaking new ground locally, picking up considerable media interest and getting a very good response from young people with whom the project had traditionally had very little relationship. One of the projects, the counselling helpline, was also attracting interest from a neighbouring local authority which expressed an interest in developing a similar service.

In the **cash cows** quadrant were the main activities that operated on a week-to-week basis. Over the past five years they had changed little and as far as the organisation was concerned would continue to serve a useful purpose. One of the activities, the arts project, was causing concern. It was attracting fewer young people and starting to drift. Its funder had described it as 'becoming rather predictable'.

The **dogs** quadrant had two activities that were part of the agency's history. The residential centre, a cottage, was donated to the agency ten years ago. At that time it was, for a short period, a 'star'. For the past two years, it had needed considerable repairs, a new roof and regular visits from the agency's administrator. As a result, it drained resources and because of the poor state of repair few groups ever visited. The international exchange programme had become an annual commitment that the agency had because it had 'done it last year'. Few people participated; it often went over-budget and took up considerable staff time. However, those who did participate thought that it was very valuable.

The portfolio analysis highlighted six strategic choices for the agency:

1. *Innovation is an important role for us. How much time and money can we risk in square 1? How much time should we give to new ideas to establish them?*
2. *What future is there for the two projects in square 2? Could they peak? What if funders were to lose interest (move onto other stars), but expectation from service users continued to rise?*
3. *Are we really confident that the items in square 3 are steady and safe?*
4. *What do we need to do with the arts project? How do we stop it drifting into square 4?*
5. *What future do we envisage for the residential centre? Do we invest in it, market it and give it a new direction or do we look to dispose of it?*
6. *Should we continue with the international exchanges? If we move out of this area will we get opposition from those of our members who benefit from it? Could we float it off to someone more skilled in this area?*

Comparing mission and activity

Case study: the Caldew Neighbourhood Project

As part of its planning day, the Caldew Neighbourhood Project reviewed its six activities against its two main purposes: 1) providing educational opportunities for those who have missed out and 2) tackling poverty. This is what they came up with.

Activity	Are we succeeding against our mission:	
	To provide educational opportunities for those who have missed out	To tackle poverty
Running an open-to-all computer room	Possibly, but is it just a recreational space for young people?	Possibly: is it providing a resource for those excluded from technology? Should the activity be refocused on those who have had least opportunity to develop technological skills?
Providing an outreach base for the College to run an adult education programme	Yes, but does it really bring in hard-to-reach groups?	Possibly in the longer term by helping people develop confidence and skills.
Running three healthy-living groups	Yes, the sessions are targeted at hard-to-reach groups and participation has been good.	Yes, there is a proven link between poor health and poverty.
Running and supporting an adult literacy group	Yes, we consistently attract people who have not participated in education or training.	Yes: overcomes a clear block to social inclusion.
Providing office space for councillors, the housing department and the Job Centre to run open sessions	Not sure: are we just being used as a convenient outpost? Need to review how our space is being used to provide opportunities for those who have missed out. Either we ensure the sessions provide this service or we make better use of our limited space.	Possibly, if being run correctly: satellite sessions should increase people's access to these agencies' services.
Providing meeting space and support for local clubs and societies.	Not sure, we need to make these various groups feel that they are an important part of the whole project so that their club or society can flourish.	Not sure. Is using the space in this manner the best way of achieving our mission of tackling poverty?

They went on to consider the following questions:

- How clear is our purpose or mission? Is it so vague that everything can be made to fit? Are we spread too thin? Do we need a sharper focus?
- Is there a clear rationale for running these activities? Do they fit with our mission? Are we the most appropriate people to run them?
- What are we driven by?

See page 104 to try this exercise.

The key strengths and weaknesses of the organisation

Part of the analysis needs to look at how the organisation is organised and operates. Questions to consider include:

- Is the organisation flexible enough to respond to changes and uncertainties?
- Does the way you are organised and work fit with your values and what you want to do?
- Do all aspects of the organisation fit together and create a coherent whole?

The management consultancy firm McKinsey & Company developed a useful framework for taking stock of an organisation. They argue that for an organisation to be effective it has to achieve a synergy between seven elements, all of which helpfully begin with the letter S.

The 7-S framework

The 7-S framework, as shown in figure 6.6, can be used to identify weaknesses and shortcomings in how an organisation works.

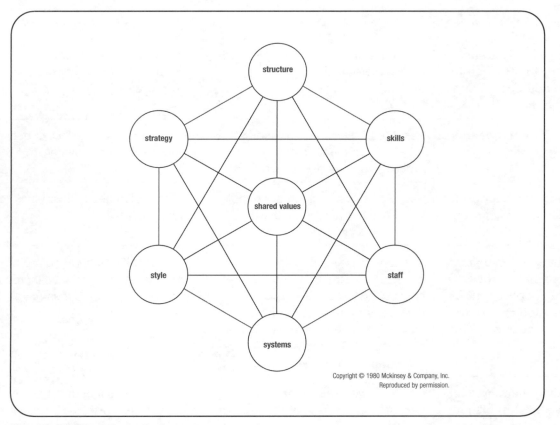

Copyright © 1980 Mckinsey & Company, Inc.
Reproduced by permission.

Fig. 6.6   The 7-S framework

Strategy

- Does the organisation have a clear purpose?
- How will the organisation evolve for the future?
- Do people in it understand its strategy?

Structure

- Do people understand how the authority relationships in the organisation work?
- Does the division of work make sense?

- Is the structure flexible enough?
- Does it allow good communication between people?

Staff

- Are the right sort of people in the right sort of jobs?
- Does the organisation have a diverse mix of people?
- Are people captured in the narrow thinking of a particular population within the organisation?

Skills

- Do people have the right mix of skills for the organisation to develop in the way that is wanted?
- Are there any current skills gaps in the organisation?
- How are current staff invested in? How are people's skills developed?
- Are there any skills needed which should be outsourced?

Systems

- Is there sufficient management control over resources?
- Is the cost of everything known?
- How are decisions made?

Style

- What is the relationship with service users like?
- Does the organisation present the kind of image that is desired?
- Does the organisation's working culture support what it is trying to do?

Shared values

- Are the organisation's shared values clear?
- Is there a clear agreement about what is important and how people behave?
- What is the organisation trying to achieve?

Learning from others: benchmarking

Benchmarking is the process of comparing how your organisation's processes and results compare with similar organisations or agreed best practice. Organisations agree to share their experience and compare their approach.

Different aspects can be benchmarked:

- **Performance:** organisations compare results and a league table of comparable performance is developed.
- **Process:** organisations compare how they manage or handle key processes or working practices.
- **Function:** organisations compare how they manage and organise internal functions.
- **Strategy:** organisations agree to share and compare current business strategy.

Benchmarking can be organised in a formal way; for example, a group of housing providers could compare key performance measures such as the management of void property levels. In formal benchmarking arrangements, organisations agree what they will disclose and the ways information will be used. Formal benchmarking leads to a league table where organisations can show their current performance.

Benchmarking can also be organised in a more informal way. For example, a group of practitioners from different organisations agree to meet to discuss how they handle a particular service delivery issue and compare what works and what does not.

Benchmarking can have several roles in the analysis stage of planning. In the benchmarking process your organisation is measured against others to give some useful pointers as to where there might be gaps or areas for improvement. It can also encourage staff to identify new and emerging ideas and to think innovatively. One participant described benchmarking as the 'organised theft of other people's ideas'. For it to work it does need an agreement to share information and experience in the belief that it will create mutual gain.

A director of a charity summarised his experience of using benchmarking:

> *After years of informal contact I managed to persuade a small group of similar organisations to take part in a benchmarking exercise. We picked on a few live issues such as volunteer development, business sponsorship and IT system management. Relevant groups of staff met to agree what they wanted to look at in each area and then organised a process of information exchange, field visits and joint seminars. I think that the process has worked very well. It has introduced people to new ideas and has provided useful ideas for improvement and future development that have gone into our business plan. In many ways seeing something similar to what you do gives you a different perspective and makes you start asking 'why do we do it like that?', which is a good starting point for future strategy.*

✎ Exercise: a SWOT analysis

Set out the strengths and weaknesses of your organisation as you see them. Note possible opportunities and threats which may emerge in the future.

Strengths	Weaknesses
Opportunities	**Threats**

✎ Exercise: predicting change

Use this exercise to identify the different kinds of change that your organisation is experiencing or is about to experience. See page 75 for some examples and explanations, and page 76 for a real-life example of how this exercise has been used.

Imposed change: a crisis – something that has to be done	External change: any predictions or possible changes in the environment	Proactive change: your organisation's strategy – where you want to be	Organisational and cultural change: your organisation's behaviour, style and way of organising

Analysis

Which of the changes are really significant?	
Can any issues be clustered together?	
Is there a logical order in which you should tackle them; i.e. is one dependent on another?	
Do you need to be proactive and strategic to avoid simply responding to other people's agenda?	

✎ Exercise: predicting trends and developments

	Next 12 months	1–3 years	Longer term
Available resources			
Changes in practice and how we work			
Changes in demand and needs			
Changes in the political or economic arena			
Changes in the environment and market			

✏️ Exercise: looking outside

In the first column list all the organisations that do similar work to yours. Then consider the similarities and differences between you and them. Then describe the current relationship and finally any ideas for how the relationship might develop.

Organisation to compare	Similarities to us	Differences from us	Current relationship	Strategic possibilities

✎ Exercise: comparing resources and results

The aim of this exercise is to work out whether the level of input invested in any activity or project corresponds to the degree of successful outputs and outcomes. So, for example, if you are using a large amount of resources on an activity, are the outputs and outcomes correspondingly large? Here is a quick reminder of the definitions outlined in Chapter 5:

- **Inputs** are the resources needed, including money, staff and volunteer time and equipment.
- **Outputs** are the activities or services that your organisation has delivered.
- **Outcomes** are the difference that your organisation makes. Outcomes should relate to the vision and benefit the organisation's service users.

Ideally, this exercise should be based on data, objective evidence and clear performance monitoring. In reality, however, organisations often do not have all of this in place and so the exercise will require some judgements to be made.

There are five stages to the exercise which can be filled out in the following table.

Matching resources and outputs/outcomes		
Stage 1: list the organisation's main activities and projects	Stage 2: assess outputs for each activity or project over the past few years and consider level of success	Stage 3: list the inputs used to deliver each activity

Analysis: how does our use of inputs compare with our outputs? Are there any activities that take up lots of resources, but deliver no or hardly any outputs? Are there any outputs that we delivered which did not involve many inputs?

Plan ahead: ideas and issues for future strategies

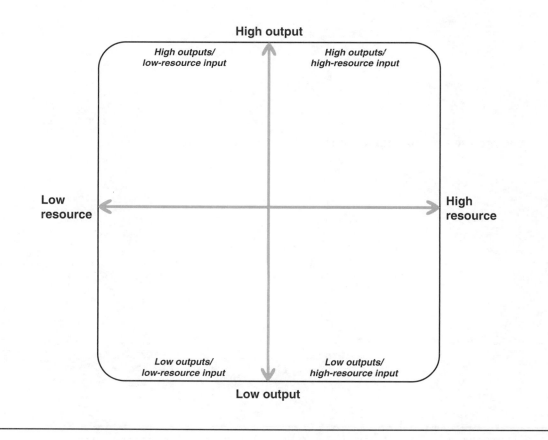

Exercise: your organisation's development stage

How would you characterise your organisation's current stage of development?

What are the key organisational issues that need to be tackled?

What are the key management issues that need to tackled?

✏️ Exercise: a portfolio matrix for your organisation

At the start of this exercise, it is useful to discuss by which criteria each activity is being valued and which factors make an activity succeed or fail.

- Question marks: new ideas, start-ups and pilots – innovative but not yet proven.
- Stars: strong, dynamic and successful projects.
- Cash cows: reliable and steady activities.
- Dogs: activities that take up resources but produce little return or value.

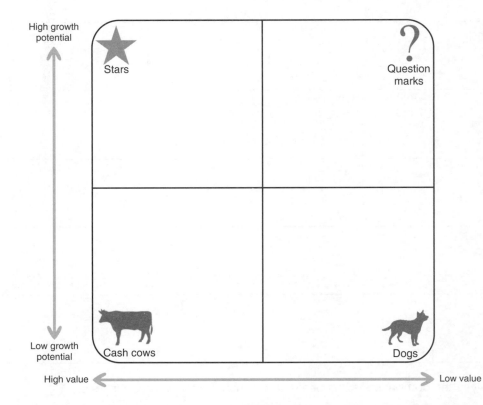

What do you think of the balance of the portfolio? How are different activities developing and what are the critical issues for each activity?

✎ Exercise: comparing mission and activity

This exercise aims to help your organisation compare its activities (services, programmes and projects) with its intended purpose and mission.

Activity	Are we succeeding against our mission?	

To analyse the comparisons it is useful to discuss the following questions:

How clear is our purpose or mission? Is it so vague that everything can be made to fit? Are we spread too thin? Do we need a sharper focus?

Is there a clear rationale for why we run these activities? Do they fit with our mission? Are we the most appropriate people to run them?

What are we driven by?

Chapter seven

Developing options and setting the strategic direction

The greater danger for most of us is not that our aim is too high, and that we might miss it, but that it is too low and we reach it.

Michelangelo

After clarifying what the organisation is for, taking stock of its development to date, and reviewing the external context, the planning process can now move on to developing options, testing choices and setting the strategic direction. Setting the direction is the point at which the analysis needs to end and the consultation and participation elements of the process draw to a close.

This chapter looks at the following issues:

1. establishing the assumptions behind the plan;
2. clarifying the organisation's limits;
3. proposing ideas for developing the organisation overall and identifying strategic choices;
4. putting forward ideas for developing the organisation's activities and evaluating these ideas;
5. agreeing and setting a strategic direction;
6. managing funding in relation to the strategic direction.

Establishing the assumptions behind the plan

Any planning process involves making some assumptions upon which planning can be based. A business plan should set out its central assumptions, as readers might wish to know the assumptions upon which the rest of the plan is based. One approach which can help organisations to set out their assumptions is to list the key ones under a series of headings:

Assumptions	Examples of assumptions made
Demand and needs	● Referrals will stay at the same rate over the next two years. ● Demand for respite care will continue to rise.
External developments	● The local authorities will increasingly move towards individual-based or user-based contracts. ● Other agencies which work in this field will continue to charge a similar fee to ours.
Internal developments	● We will still be able to recruit, support and retain a volunteer team at its current level. ● Staff turnover will remain at its current level.
Financial	● For the next two years increases in fee rates will meet inflation and pay awards. ● Our fundraising income will rise by 5% each year for the next three years.

Case study: testing your assumptions

The Woodley Centre provided a well-established specialist advice and advocacy service. As part of its strategic planning process the staff and trustees identified five assumptions that people in the organisation seemed to hold. After discussion they went on to test and challenge each assumption and then to identify which actions to take.

Assumption	Testing and challenging the assumption	Action
Our main funder (the local council) will continue to support us.	• Do we know what they are planning? Cuts or commissioning? • Next May's local elections could be a close contest and could lead to political change. • Some of the staff we work closely with at the council are likely to leave.	• Ensure that we don't take the council's support for granted. • Plan to build stronger and deeper individual relationships with key officers and elected members. • Produce regular material showcasing our work.
We will be able to maintain the same level of volunteer workers.	• We have always been able to recruit over the past ten years. • It is likely that some longstanding volunteers might retire/leave over the next few years.	• Increase awareness of the danger of being complacent and taking our volunteers for granted. • Start a volunteer development programme to encourage volunteers to stay. • Plan a recruitment campaign.
Levels of demand for our service will be the same or will increase.	• All indicators suggest that this will be the case unless something major happens, such as the establishment of another organisation doing the same work.	• Need to plan for demand to increase and consider the organisational implications. • Monitor possible competition.
We will be the main provider for this kind of service locally.	• No obvious alternative, although some private firms might start to offer this service.	• Monitor possible competition.
Our service will remain relevant to those who use it.	• Danger of assuming that just because we have a waiting list we must be doing the right thing. • Do we really know what our service users want and need? • What about unmet need or people who can't get through to us?	• Do a service user survey and consultation exercise to collect their views. • Identify unmet needs.

Assumptions need to be credible, discussed openly and periodically checked. It is common to continue operating as normal under an assumption which in fact no longer applies, such as 'our services will always be needed' or 'supporters will keep backing us'. It is useful, therefore, to look for factors that might contradict or challenge the assumption and to test how safe it is. It is worthwhile considering what the organisation would need to do if the assumption turns out to be wrong.

Case study: scenario planning

A housing organisation used its annual staff residential day to consider three potential scenarios:

1. The decision by a major funder to withdraw its financial commitment by phasing it out over two years.

2. A change in the political control and the managerial style within a local authority. The new leadership would be interested in partnerships and transferring the management of several projects from the public to the independent sectors.

3. A decline in demand. A combination of reasons has led to a sharp fall in the numbers of referrals to a usually busy project. Financial, marketing and service plans need to be implemented quickly.

Staff worked in teams to suggest short-term and long-term action plans, explore options, spot dangers and test out the organisation's current processes. Extensive discussion followed about how the scenarios could have been anticipated or avoided, the importance of a coordinated response throughout the organisation and the need for contingency plans.

The outcome of the day was that all staff had some experience of strategic thinking, and several outline contingency plans were produced (for example blueprints for possible projects should the opportunity arise).

Three months after the exercise, a similar situation to one of the scenarios did arise which tested the effectiveness of the plans and the process.

Clarifying the organisation's limits

All organisations have limits. Discussion of organisational strategy without reference to the organisation's limits is pointless day-dreaming. There are different sorts of limits: some are fixed and others are more negotiable.

Possible limits include:

- **Physical:** 'Our current office could only cope with one more member of staff.'
- **Legal and constitutional:** 'Moving into this area of work could take us beyond our legal powers as a charity.'
- **Level of manageable risk:** 'To run this number of innovative and pioneering projects would be unacceptable to our trustees.'
- **Human:** 'Our current staff team is not skilled in this area of work.'
- **Resource:** 'To develop in such a way would stretch our management and communication systems.'
- **Financial:** 'To continue with this kind of funding would seriously harm our cash flow.'

Once you have identified the limiting factors it is helpful to consider the following questions:

1. How fixed is each limiting factor?

2. What creates the limiting factor?

3. What would you have to do to change it?

Usually the most obvious limits are the resource or financial ones. However, it is interesting to look at how an organisation's traditions, practices and long-term commitments can also be a limiting factor. Indeed, many limiting factors are the direct product of the organisation's history. Indeed, these are the types of limits that need to be addressed and possibly challenged when they interfere in the progress of an organisation, as outlined in the following case study.

A useful exercise to help analyse all types of limits is to consider how the organisation would be different if it were to be created today. What would the organisation look like? Which services would be provided? What would the relationship to service users be like? Some organisations have adopted a technique called 'zero-based budgeting': managers rebuild the budget for each activity as if they were starting it again (see page 144). The case for expenditure and staff time has to be justified against the organisation's strategy. As a result of this exercise, many limiting factors can be challenged and previously committed resources can be subsequently redirected to other priorities.

Case study: a limit on strategy

The honeymoon period in Kerry's new job as development manager for a charity for people with learning difficulties did not last long. She had been employed to research, design and set up new projects and initiatives. The charity desperately needed to improve its services and develop a commitment to service-user involvement. In her first few months, she developed proposals for three small projects. At first the reaction of her colleagues was very supportive.

Every six months, managers met for a planning day. The bulk of Kerry's first meeting was given over to consideration of her proposals. None of the managers present disagreed in principle with the proposals. However, each proposal was subject to detailed examination of the potential risk, the financial implications and the other costs. Kerry agreed to produce further reports and feasibility studies.

Three months later, all the projects were starting to slide off the drawing board. However much extra information she produced, the projects were still being deferred.

Kerry fully understood that all new proposals needed to be reviewed rigorously. However, she felt frustrated that many of the charity's current services were poor or in decline, but were never subject to any kind of review at all. Some were even at odds with the charity's recent statement of values. Once projects had been established and were up and running they carried on being allocated resources every year regardless.

Kerry resolved to highlight these concerns robustly at the next management meeting. She was worried that she might encounter a negative reaction, but, while some people were naturally defensive, her fresh perspective alerted the team to how the organisation had become stuck in its ways and was limiting its own progress. By the end of the meeting, they had agreed to conduct a review of the organisation's existing services and to assist Kerry in achieving the crucial outcomes that she had been employed to deliver.

Ideas for developing the organisation

All organisations have options available to them. Doing nothing new is one choice. Identifying choices and options for the future should be a participatory process that involves all individuals (see Chapter 4 for advice on consultation).

Identifying strategic choices

In *The Strategic Planning Workbook*, psychologist and management strategist, Neville Lake, describes four key choices in working out future possibilities for organisations.

Future choices:	
Choice 1	• Stay the same • Consolidate • Keep doing what we do
Choice 2	• Grow • Expand • Become a bigger player
Choice 3	• Develop new projects • Diversify • Think innovatively
Choice 4	• Take on a new role or focus • Reinvent • Try a different model

The model can be used to stimulate discussion within voluntary organisations about what sort of strategy might be possible. Here are the choices with some additional material which sets out some of the issues and risks involved and also some examples of how some organisations have followed each option.

Choice 1: staying the same 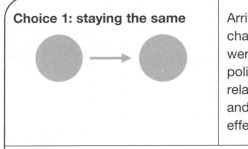	Arriving at their annual awayday, the staff and trustees of a children's charity felt battle-weary. It seemed that every three months they were being required to jump through new hoops and respond to new policies, directions and external change. The group immediately related to this option. The charity desperately needed some stability and time to consolidate. It felt confident that its services were effective and much in need. Why change for the sake of it?

Taking this option can provide the space to consolidate and improve services and avoids organisations chasing things simply because they are new. It might seem tempting because stability and continuing business as usual is attractive to those organisations with lots of challenges. However, it also assumes that the world outside the organisation (needs, funding, policies, etc.) will remain stable.

Choice 2: growth 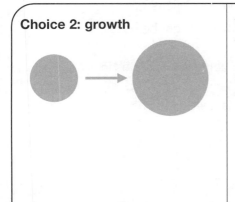	The management team of a housing association recognised that over the past five to ten years they had followed this model of growth, although they had never formally adopted it. The association had been keen to expand, move into new areas and diversify by keenly following up business and funding opportunities, taking up or merging with other associations and moving into new geographic areas. In many ways this felt good. The association proudly boasted of its year-on-year growth. The team felt that it had been able to meet more gaps in housing provision and social need. Managers felt good (and were better rewarded) about leading a growing organisation.

The decision to choose this option can be driven by different motives: a commitment to deliver more services to people or communities who need them, a view that growing could create a stronger and more sustainable organisation, or a competitive urge to become bigger. This option is credible if there is a clear level of unmet demand and need.

The key challenges that can be faced when going down this route are about ensuring that:

- significant growth will be sustainable (what is the risk of failure when short-term funding ends?);
- the prospects for growth fit within the overall vision, mission and values;
- the organisation has (or can quickly get) the necessary skills, expertise and organisational capacity to support new development.

Choice 3: diversification 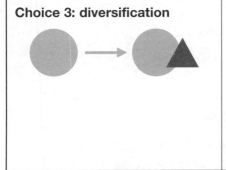	The manager of a service for young people with learning disabilities developed an idea for a project that would fill a much-needed gap in provision for clients aged 16 and over. She produced a business case for the service to set up a picture framing business: a social enterprise that would provide work and/or training for around ten young adult clients. Moving into this was a new venture for the service, but it met a need and fitted with other activities. In time it became a useful income stream. (See page 118 for information on business cases and page 115 on social enterprise.)

This strategy can be a way of encouraging innovation and moving into new areas that can revitalise the organisation. Additional projects need to be fully costed to ensure that the direct and indirect costs are clear and it is important to check that the project is in line with the organisation's overall vision and future strategy. The risks of this strategy are that new ventures can take the organisation too far outside of its area of expertise or competence and that too much time can be spent on new projects at the expense of core work.

Choice 4: reinvention 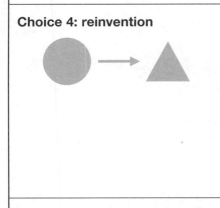	The trustees of a centre for people with disabilities felt that they had reached a crisis point. The centre kept adding projects and services to the point where the centre was now a significant local provider. Almost all resources and time were spent on keeping the centre operating and funded. At an awayday the trustees felt that they had 'lost the plot' and agreed a plan to refocus the centre on campaigning, rights and involving service users rather than seeing them as 'clients' or customers. This radical plan would involve major change and would include withdrawing from or closing down some activities in order to use resources differently.

This strategic choice is essentially about reinvention or starting again. There needs to be a real commitment to it and some enthusiasm to make it happen. Usually it will involve managing big internal and external changes, including stopping some activities. It is not for the faint-hearted.

It is useful to discuss the following questions when considering the options:

- Which of these alternatives (or possibly combinations of choices) might be possible for your organisation over the next few years?
- Based on your analysis of the organisation and the external context it operates in, which ones feel right?
- Which risks are involved and what key management action is needed to ensure the strategy's success?

There could be an additional, fifth choice:

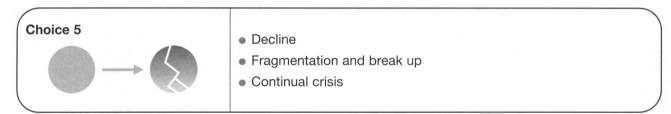

Choice 5

- Decline
- Fragmentation and break up
- Continual crisis

This 'choice' often comes about by neglect or leaving things to chance. The organisation declines gradually and lurches from crisis to crisis. What can be done to avoid this?

A useful approach is to start by posing options for the future, such as:

- Should your organisation grow, stay the same or get smaller?
- What aspects of your work should you do more or less of?
- In which geographic areas should you do more work and in which less?
- What style of work should you do more of or less of?
- Which client groups should you target?
- Should the organisation become more specialist or more generalist?
- What alliances or relationships with others should you develop?

At this stage it is helpful to bring the service users' perspective and/or the organisation's mission into the discussion. The focus of the direction needs to be on what the outside world needs and not just what feels comfortable for people in the organisation.

Case study: identifying options by using scenarios

The Community Arts Team had reached a critical point in the agreement of its future strategy. In the ten years since it had been set up it had developed a track record of running successful projects and programmes. However, the initiatives and ideas had often come from spotting a pot of money and developing a project to fit with it. The team decided it needed a strategic plan to guide its future development.

Working with a consultant, the team analysed its development to date. It reviewed past projects, looked at what other agencies were doing and identified the key external trends and opportunities. The team soon realised that it had far too many ideas about how it could develop than it could possibly manage or resource. To move the plan forward, the team developed a list of possible scenarios about how it could develop over the next three to five years.

Scenario 1: Aim to stay roughly as we are

This option assumed that the team would continue to be able to obtain funding and support to carry on with the same pattern of activities and projects.

Scenario 2: Focus on community regeneration

The team operated in an area scheduled for a major investment of government regeneration funds. This scenario would involve the team working with the newly created regeneration partnership and using art forms to involve local people, encourage feedback and also improve the urban environment.

Scenario 3: Become a community business

The team could develop a number of small to medium-scale social businesses such as an internet café, an arts venue and an education and training programme that could operate on a proper business basis. Any profit made would be used to subsidise other activities.

Scenario 4: Reduce our focus

This option would mean that the team would only work with young people. This focus would give greater cohesion to the team and was based on recognising that the team's greatest skills and competency were in working with younger people.

Scenario 5: Link up with a partner

The final option recognised that the team had developed a strong link from working with a local theatre company. In many respects their work strongly overlapped. This option would involve much more shared working, joint bidding to run projects together and sharing of some resources. A longer-term possibility of a merger would be explored.

The team presented each of the options to a special meeting of their management board. Each scenario was evaluated against the team's mission and the board's assessment of local need and possible funding. For some scenarios the board was able to do simple cost–benefit analyses, setting out possible pros and cons. Careful facilitation led the board away from attempting to try to do all of them and to a position where a number of elements from three scenarios were combined.

Participants felt that the process worked. Staff and board members felt positive that there was not just one possible way forward presented to the board. The discussion on possible scenarios had to be informed by an understanding of the changing environment that the agency operated in.

Case study: example ideas prompt worksheet

This is an example of a review sheet compiled by a communications worker in a small national charity. Her main responsibilities are keeping the charity's membership involved and informed, running the charity's information work and lobbying government.

Area of work: Communications

Are the original aims and ideas still valid?	*What has changed in this area since the last plan?*	*What are the likely key expectations and demands?*
• Yes, there is strong demand for information.	• Much greater use of the internet. • Members of the public assume that we run a free public information service. • More requests for information and advice from social workers and other professional workers. Increased complexity of enquiries – more detailed requests for information.	• Continued demand.
Over the next three years what do we think will stay the same?	*Over the next three years what do we think will be different?*	*What are the main trends and developments?*
• Many of our supporters not being online and dependent on traditional media and forms of communication.	• Likelihood of new legislation – need to encourage supporters to lobby their MP.	• Increase in lobbying and parliamentary work. • Greater use of the internet. • We get little feedback from our members' newsletter. Is it read?
What is happening in the sector?	*What ideas are there for developing this work?*	*Which decisions need to be taken?*
• Alliances are being formed on policy work. • We are seen as the lead agency locally.	• Develop an email list and internet-based discussion list for our supporters. • Can we turn passive members into active supporters, donors and lobbyists?	• How to organise, support and coordinate lobbying. • Should we move towards relying mainly on email and internet communications? • Should we develop a public information service? • Could we charge other agencies (such as local authorities) for information and advice work? • Are information, communication and lobbying too many functions for one job?

Earning money from what you do: social enterprise

In most voluntary organisations income is raised from donations, fees and payments for work done (contracts). This income is then used to fund the work. Increasingly, however, organisations are developing more complex and creative models.

Over the years, the move towards business planning and social enterprise has been one of the most talked about and talked-up issues in the voluntary sector. Examples of charities earning money and visionary social entrepreneurs are held up as examples to follow. However, voluntary organisations making money is not that new! Many organisations have traded or charged for their services in the past. The social enterprise movement, though, has given it much greater impetus and profile.

At its simplest, social enterprise is about earning money from what an organisation does or from the expertise that it has. It involves operating as a business, with services, products and customers, but with a social motive: the business should benefit the community. It can involve operating in two different but overlapping worlds: commercial and charitable.

Social enterprise can take different forms, including:

- creating a new organisation as a not-for-profit company;
- setting up or converting to a charitable incorporated organisation;
- having separate trading structures within an organisation that work alongside the mainstream charitable activities;

Social enterprise can be an organisation or an activity. People in existing organisations can be encouraged to identify for which current services some people could be charged. Examples of social enterprise include:

- direct trading ventures to the public or other 'businesses', such as operating shops, cafés, childcare services and other ventures, but with the clear distinction that profits are returned to benefit the charity;
- selling knowledge and expertise;
- charging for consultancy, training and publications;
- contracted services, such as gardening, environmental improvements and administrative support, by bidding for contracts to take on specific activities.

Any trading operation must fit with the mission, values and identity of the organisation.

Developing trading or a social enterprise can have an impact on the internal management and style of the organisation. A director of a charity that had encouraged income generation from trading commented on an effect it had on his staff:

Two years in we have had to deal with an element of internal competition. One or two people seemed to believe that their work is more important because it brought money in. They expected status and first call on things like receiving admin support.

Case study: a stalled plan for generating income

After Val's first month as director of the Meadow Centre three things were clear to her.

1. There was very strong demand for the counselling and therapy services that the Centre offered.
2. The Centre had a team of staff who were highly skilled and committed to the Centre's vision of tackling stress in society.
3. The Centre's income was too reliant on public sector grants and contracts.

Val spent time working on ideas to develop the Centre and came up with some ideas for generating income:

- Develop a sliding scale of charges for counselling work. Val estimated that the majority of clients would still get a free service, but people who could afford it would be asked to contribute.

- Deliver an employee assistance service for the staff of a large local employer who were suffering from stress (the company's human resources director had expressed interest in the Centre doing so).

- Develop a training programme in inter-personnel and communication skills.

Using her business experience, Val drew up plans for each of these services and started to introduce the idea to key trustees and staff members. Val felt confident that these proposals would secure the Centre's work and take it to a new level.

An awayday was organised to work on the Centre's future strategy. The discussion that followed a PowerPoint presentation from Val was mainly negative. Members of staff were concerned that charging would take the centre away from its founding principles of reaching out to those most disadvantaged. Would those who pay get a better service, such as the offer of convenient appointment times? One worker suggested that he might as well go into or set up a private practice. The Centre's treasurer wondered if bringing in money would simply lead to their current statutory funders reducing their support.

Talking over the session with the committee's Chair Val realised that:

- for it to work, any income venture had to fit in with the Centre's ethos and style;

- a trading venture had to be more than making money: she had not emphasised how the ideas could have extended the reach of the Centre, made it more independent and taken it into new areas of work;

- she needed to demonstrate that by earning money the Centre would be able to create an income stream that it could use to work with the most disadvantaged clients, hard-to-reach groups or 'unpopular' causes that their current funders ignored. Trading could help the Centre to achieve its original mission.

This case study shows that although you may come across objections to social enterprise ideas, if a proposed venture is presented in a way that demonstrates how it furthers the organisation's mission and fits with its values and ethos, people can understand the logic for trading. Indeed, there are several compelling reasons for developing income-generating schemes:

- **To create an unrestricted income stream:** by generating its own income, an organisation can create income that is not dependent on the changing policies of funders. Income from trading can give an organisation money that is not restricted and does not have to be used for a particular purpose.

- **To broaden the funding base:** many voluntary organisations have seen social enterprise as a way of diversifying their funding and reducing their dependence on one or two main funders. This can give an organisation a renewed sense of its independence in that it is not totally reliant on one or two funders and, as such, subject to their whims.

- **To develop the organisation:** operating as a social business can raise management skills, improve marketing and build the organisation's profile.

- **As a way to meet the mission:** successful social enterprises can create jobs for intended beneficiaries and play a part in strengthening a local economy.

- **To bring in or develop a set of useful skills and processes:** this includes developing skills such as market research, marketing, risk management and financial control and planning. It will help ensure that management and business systems are sound.

Getting started on social enterprise

The first thing to find out is whether the organisation's constitution allows this kind of activity. In broad terms, charity law allows trading if it advances the charity's primary purposes. The organisation's governing document needs to be examined and options such as creating a separate trading arm considered.

If trading is an option, as with any business idea, you have to be clear that the organisation has or could have something of value that other people or organisations would be prepared to pay for. This often comes from recognising the strengths of the organisation and being able to turn them into services or products. The business idea need not be a tangible product (selling products). It could be about the organisation's expertise or knowledge: its know-how.

Furthermore, you will need to consider whether the organisation has the right kind of management, marketing and business skills. Can existing skills such as fundraising be developed into the skills involved in running a business?

It is important to spend time looking at the market that the enterprise will operate in. Finding out what other people do and comparing what else is on offer should help you to analyse:

- how the market works: how big is it and who buys and when?
- who else is in the market: what is the nature of the competition?

The answers to these questions can help to define what the organisation intends to offer and also identify the best ways it can be marketed. In developing an idea for income generation or for a social enterprise it is useful to draw up a business case.

Case study: recognising valuable skills

The manager of a medium-sized charity commented:

It wasn't until we started thinking about social enterprise that we realised how much we gave away to agencies and people who were not our intended users and in some cases could afford to pay, and also what valuable skills we had within our organisation.

In the past we shied away from asking to be paid properly for what we do. A couple of years ago we developed a new and innovative way of working with our client group. After some good publicity, we started getting requests from people to visit us or to see our materials, or to speak at conferences. All we ever got in cash terms was travel expenses! We gave away our expertise. We could have packaged it or even developed a franchise.

We are now developing training, publications and consultancy services. We now try to see our knowledge and expertise as a key asset.

Evaluating ideas

The list of options for developing the organisation probably will be more than the organisation can deal with, so some clear criteria are needed to evaluate possible choices. It is advisable to work through the following four points in relation to each possibility that emerges:

1. What is (or should be) distinctive about your organisation? Does this option fit with your mission and values?

2. What are you effective at? What do you do consistently well? Is your expertise best suited to this option?

3. What are your organisation's priorities? Which needs are most important to meet? Does this option fit with your priorities?

4. Will this option be financially viable or, if not, is it important enough to be subsidised? Will you be able to succeed?

The above criteria can be applied to each option and be graded accordingly. This should allow you to reject a number of them. Others can be combined into groups and then narrowed down to a workable number of strategic aims which will become the main driving force of the organisation.

Ideas for developing activities

Business cases

The term 'business case' is used increasingly within voluntary organisations. A business case is often required by senior management to set out and justify why a new project, idea or venture should go ahead and why resources should be allocated to it. Some public sector agencies also request business cases in considering new ventures or whether to commission new services. Used in this way, a business case is an argument for why a decision-maker should support a project or action and summarises the reasons and potential value for initiating, backing or investing in it. If agreed, the new venture would become part of the bigger organisation.

A business case should set out the reason for doing something, review the assumptions and risks involved, show the likely benefits and costs and any other implications for doing it. It should be brief, outline the key arguments, enabling potential supporters to understand the idea, and show that the idea has been considered properly.

A business case is different from a traditional funding pitch. It needs to show that by investing resources, value will be created.

To analyse a business idea you can focus on:

- **the durability of the idea:** is it a sustainable business idea or is it based on an unproved market?
- **full costing:** is the idea fully costed? How have overhead costs such as accommodation and management support been planned? Is there a danger that the main organisation will provide a 'hidden subsidy' to the trading venture?

A typical format for a business case

Section	Content	Key points
A description of the problem or opportunity	• What problem or gap the business case is trying to deal with or what opportunity you propose to take advantage of.	• The context and background. • The intended outcomes and how they fit with the current strategic/business plan.
An outline of what is being proposed	• What you intend to do: a short description of the project or service you would like to run.	• The reasons why the project or service will deliver the outcomes.
Cost and resource implications	• How much will it all cost? • What will your organisation be expected to contribute to it? • How will it be funded?	• Fully cost all activities to ensure that all direct and indirect costs are included.
Expected benefits	• What will the project or service deliver?	• Outputs and outcomes
Organisational implications	• How will the new project or service fit within the organisation?	• The reasons why you are the right people to do it.
Assessment of potential value and gain	• A summary of the overall value of the project or service and how it fits with your mission and values.	• Also include the implications of not doing it.

Case study: appraising possible projects

At their annual planning day, the management committee and staff of a community development agency discussed four potential initiatives and ideas that the agency could become involved in. Each idea was tested against six criteria.

- Does it fit with our stated mission and core values?
- Is there a definite need for it?
- Does it fit with our strategy?
- Is it sustainable? That is, does it have a long-term future?

- Do we have the capacity – the skills, expertise, and physical space – to run it?
- Will the project's direct and indirect costs be covered? In other words, will it be funded on a full cost recovery basis?

	Possible new idea			
Criteria	Working with the local crime prevention partnership	Setting up a food co-operative selling healthy foods	Opening up an internet café	Helping to set up a local credit union
Fits with our mission and values?	Yes, provided it genuinely involves local people.	Yes, it fits with combating poverty and improving health.	Yes, it supports access to education.	Yes, it fits with combating poverty.
Is there a definite need for it?	A recent community survey shows that fear of crime is growing.	The survey highlights that this is a key issue.	Not sure. We would need to investigate whether there is a real and proven need.	Yes – the advice centre reports an upward trend in debt.
Does it fit with our strategy?	This is relevant to our mission but would be a new area for us and would be (yet another) strategic priority.	Yes, supporting locally run initiatives is a key priority.	Hard to see how it fits into our current priorities.	Yes, supporting locally run initiatives is a key priority.
Is it sustainable?	Don't know – funding for the partnership has only been agreed for the next year.	If successful it would be; if not, it could develop into a social business with a declining need for external funding.	There is a prospect of initial funding but no guarantee of revenue support and replacement costs.	Experience elsewhere suggests that if it builds up sufficient members it could be viable in three to five years.
Do we have the capacity to run it?	Yes, but would take up staff time.	Yes – we have successfully supported similar initiatives.	Yes, but it would mean reorganising office space.	Yes – initially we could house it and offer support.
Will the project's direct and indirect costs be covered?	Not all – our staff time involved in participating in the partnership is unlikely to be reimbursed.	Yes – it would be fully costed and treated as a separate cost centre.	Not sure; we would need to look into revenue support and replacement costs.	Yes. It would also need to be on a full cost recovery basis.

Case study: let's just keep doing it

The management committee of a community development initiative soon hit a difficult conversation at their strategy awayday.

The organisation's mission was to help to build a strong community life, encourage volunteering and increase opportunities in the district.

The vice chair described the problem:

> For the past fifteen years we have organised a summer festival. The aims of the festival were never really spelled out, but it is supposed to bring people together, showcase the skills that we have in the community and raise some much needed money.

> At the awayday our treasurer was very clear about the problem. She produced charts showing that for the past six years the festival has been in terminal decline. Fewer people attend and participate. The numbers of volunteers involved have dropped and it has shifted from being an income stream to something that costs us a lot to run.

> The discussion that followed was revealing. Some people went all nostalgic about how brilliant the festival had been in the past. Others had ideas to revitalise it (that other people could do). In the end the discussion faded out with a vague statement to keep it under review and an appeal for volunteers to work on it.

> Maybe it's part of our culture that we see things coming to an end as a failure. Perhaps we just need to accept that some activities do reach the end of the line and that bringing them to an end might release time and resources for new things to replace them. I just wonder how bad the festival has to become before we will do something!

If you have activities or services that do not fit with your organisation's purpose it is useful to consider the following questions.

- Could it be that our stated purpose is out of date or no longer relevant to service users?
- Why are we doing this?
  - Is it a historical accident?
  - Have we just drifted into it?
  - Are we the best people to do it?

The strategic direction

Making the decision about which strategic direction to take can be a tough call. It is easy to avoid clear decisions, say 'yes' to everything and produce a plan that lacks focus, clarity and realism. As such, strategic management at this stage in the process is often about deciding what not to do as much as what to do. It can be a difficult challenge to reject activities and projects that seem potentially valuable, but it is necessary to do so if any given activity is likely to overstretch the organisation.

It is also important to ensure at this point that you do not become too involved in detail or funding issues. The organisation needs to have the confidence and independence to say what it wants to do and *then* look at the detail of how to implement and fund it.

Finally, it is useful to keep in mind that there is a balance to be struck between setting a strategic direction that is challenging and demanding and one that will be relatively easy to deliver. This question of balance was commented on by the chair of trustees of a community association:

> *It's a real strength of our organisation that we have so many different ideas and views on how we should develop. Our last planning session produced fourteen ideas of what we could do over the next three years. Some of them, like opening a food co-op or starting an older volunteers' group were quite exciting. Compared to the public sector organisation that I work in, the level of innovation and energy is much higher. However, it also poses a real challenge. We are not very good at saying 'no'. Sometimes we commit to things that we know we will struggle to deliver and then as a consequence we spread ourselves too thin.*

> *I have learnt that it's my job to slow the process down and make sure that we are realistic without killing enthusiasm and energy. I have to keep saying that it is better to do three things well than attempt to do six things badly.*

The following case study shows how the strategic direction keeps an organisation in touch with external developments and change.

Same mission – different strategic aims

In 1986, health workers, community activists and people infected by HIV came together in a Midlands town to create an organisation to do something about the issue. After years of hard work raising the profile of the issue, running HIV awareness courses and providing practical support to people with HIV, the group held an awayday to review progress. A key goal of the day was to review the organisation's mission:

> *To support people infected and affected by the disease and to overcome the ignorance and prejudice that surround it.*

The organisation's history could be described in three phases.

1. **Early days:** the organisation was driven by a feeling of impending crisis. It was primarily volunteer-led and grew very quickly. The organisation was informal, flexible and grabbed opportunities.

2. **Early to late 1990s:** staff were appointed to deliver a range of personal care, support and advocacy services to service users, and a training programme was developed and delivered to key groups and communities.

3. **New phase:** a strong sense of change was caused by the development of drug regimes that kept infected people alive, a reduced public profile about the disease and changes in funding practices. A new strategic direction was agreed that would focus much more on helping people to live with the disease, provide information about drug treatment and also take education and prevention work into the mainstream.

One of the original founding members commented that the original mission was still relevant, but that the organisation's strategic aims for delivering it had needed to change and respond to the needs, demands and opportunities that existed.

Agreeing the strategic direction

To agree strategic aims and hence the strategic direction you need to continually refer to the limiting factors and the organisation's mission and values. The process involves continuous movement between generating options, making priorities and working within the limiting factors.

The mission statement is hard to measure and act on because it is a statement of intent, not necessarily of specific action. The strategic aims need to indicate the clear direction and priority of the organisation for its immediate to medium-term future. The operational objectives should subsequently focus on tasks and provide a measurable work plan for the organisation.

Experience from contact with many organisations has shown that anything more than six to seven strategic aims leads to a plan (and an organisation) that is fragmented, confused and pulling in different directions. Strategic aims need to:

- indicate a clear direction;
- be focused on intended outcomes;
- be integrated with other aims;
- be realistic and attainable.

The process of setting these strategic aims is likely to involve turning down someone's favourite project, deciding to withdraw from an area of work or shifting resources from one area to another. This will usually involve anxiety and conflict. As emphasised throughout this book, however, it is important that as much attention is paid to what the organisation is *not* going to do as to what it *is* going to do.

Writing strategies for strategic aims

Once you have set your organisation's strategic aims, some strategies will need to be drawn up to break down the outcomes, key measures (i.e. measuring performance and results), outputs, work plans, costings and resources, and review points/progress monitoring.

A template for this is set out on page 135. The template can form the basis of the business plan and also lead on to individual and operational work planning.

There is a danger that senior managers will write too much of the plan. Clearly trustees and managers have the overall responsibility for the mission and agreeing the strategic aims, but if they involve themselves in the detail of the operational objectives then the plan will never properly become the property of the organisation.

The following case study gives some examples of strategic aims and operational objectives.

Case study: moving from mission to strategic aims and operational objectives

The Eastside Business Advice Agency was set up to help inner-city residents explore the possibility of becoming self-employed and creating small businesses. The agency used its vision, mission and values, as outlined below, to set out its strategic aims and operational objectives as follows.

Vision

A viable and sustainable local economy.

Mission

To provide high-quality advice, training and support to emerging or newly created small businesses.

Values

We will ensure the highest standards of quality assurance.

We will safeguard equal opportunities in all cases.

We will provide full access to all our services to emerging or newly created small businesses.

Strategic aims

The agency agreed four strategic aims to guide all of its work over the next two years.

1. Continue to provide affordable and effective advice, counselling and information services to new or potential businesses.
2. Provide a high-quality training programme for business owners in three areas: management skills, marketing and quality assurance.
3. Support cooperation between new businesses, encourage marketing of inner-city businesses and identify new business opportunities.
4. Investigate and pilot ways of supporting businesses facing insolvency.

Operational objectives

For aim 3, 'Support cooperation between new businesses, encourage marketing of inner city businesses and identify new business opportunities' there are six operational objectives:

1. Encourage three inner-city business networks through monthly breakfast seminars and quarterly business forums. The forums should aim to attract 150 participants in total (100 hours).
2. Organise four self-financing business advertisement campaigns promoting local business (30 hours).
3. Create a women's business forum that will have a minimum of 20 participants and be able to be self-managing (60 hours; to be implemented by February).
4. Organise an inner-city business exhibition; target attendance: 400 people (300 hours, planned date in October, budget: £12,000).
5. Develop and implement a strategy to raise funds for a food purchasing and distribution cooperative (75 hours; first report to January management committee).
6. Participate in the management committee of the electronic village steering group (45 hours).

The operational objectives were produced by the relevant team member. They estimated how much time they would spend on each item as an indicator of priorities. The operational objectives then became the work plan for each staff member.

Ways to avoid setting the strategic direction

To set priorities, make choices and decide which direction to go in, you need to make clear and determined decisions. This can often cause anxiety and conflict and will require sustained commitment and leadership.

Here are some ways that boards and managers can avoid making strategic decisions.

1. **Ask for more consultation.** Avoid making a decision until every possible interested party or stakeholder has had their say and been 'consulted to death'. At the end of the process people will be so bored with talking about it and endless consultation that the strategy will wither away.

2. **Do a little of everything.** Rather than accepting that resources are limited and you can't do everything, try to dabble a bit in all things. Commit to doing eight things badly rather than five things well.

3. **Refuse to give up things.** Some things have reached the end of their natural life. Rather than allowing and planning for the closure – prolong the agony and keep them going.

4. **Say 'yes' to everything.** In the interests of creativity and participation back every project and say yes to every new idea or proposal. Someone else can sort out the details later.

5. **Ask for lots of information.** Keep asking for risk analysis, detailed forecasts and projections to be done – eventually people will give up.

6. **Add things on.** Make a clear strategic choice about what you intend to do and then add a few small things in as well.

7. **Take on something without the resources to do it.** Say that you are going to do something and launch it in the full knowledge that you do not have the resources, skills and expertise to do it properly. Something will turn up.

8. **Do it on the cheap.** Ignore the full cost of it. Cut corners.

Ten ways in which funding can distort your strategic direction

It is important to ensure that the need for funding and income generation, although part of the strategic process, does not dominate when you are setting the strategic direction. Here are ten ways in which the wrong kind of funding can distort your organisation's strategy and even damage the organisation.

1. **It's all about short-termism.** Year-to-year funding scrambles make long-term planning hard. The organisation lacks security and finds it hard to recruit and retain staff. A lot of work goes into starting projects and activities but an absence of any long-term funding means that they never really deliver their potential.

2. **Capital rich – revenue poor.** Going for a capital project such as a new building can create a major focus for fundraising effort. In the enthusiasm to raise the capital amount, the annual running costs are often underestimated or overlooked.

3. **No-one pays for the centre.** Many funding bodies are keen to fund projects and specific programmes rather than simply give grants to an organisation. This can create an organisational imbalance: new work is developed, but the organisation's

infrastructure and management systems are not sufficient to support and service them.

4. **Cash flow is crucial.** It is not just about how much you get from a funder but also when you get it. Having to chase money and dealing with uneven patterns of income and expenditure (such as spending most of the money in the first half of the year, but not being paid until the third quarter) can test an organisation's management and financial capacity.

5. **Strings are attached.** Sometimes funders will attach restrictions as to how a fund can be spent or earmark it for a particular purpose. A problem occurs if meeting such directions distorts the work of the organisation. Workers at a youth development agency noted that their work was being directed to work with 18- to 24-year-olds as that group was seen as being a priority to funders. Other groups that the agency considered a priority were being ignored.

6. **They won't last for ever.** Most capital purchases (buildings, equipment, vehicles) will need either replacing with new ones or, at the very least, repairing and upgrading. They usually depreciate in value.

7. **Fast growth.** Growth can be hard to manage. The rapid expansion of an organisation's services and activities needs to be matched with significant growth in the organisation's management capacity and ability.

8. **Uneven growth.** Sometimes one aspect of an organisation's work becomes attractive to funders and therefore money starts to pour into it. It radiates success and prestige, making it tempting to focus all energy and effort into it. This can cause problems for other parts of the organisation. Care is needed to ensure that long-term work is not lost because a particular area of work has become flavour of the month.

9. **High management costs.** Some forms of funding have high transaction costs. Funders expect regular monitoring reports, performance measures, audit returns and other management tasks. The cost and time of such tasks needs to be recognised and budgeted for.

10. **Arriving somewhere you don't want to be.** Funding can often take you down a path to somewhere that you did not want to go to. Over a three-year period, a community regeneration project noticed its work changing from community development to running vocational training courses. The project leader said that 'a pot of money became available to open up access routes back to college – we applied for it and were successful. Although some good work has been done, it has shifted our focus, changed our culture and our relationship to our service users – we never wanted to be a mini college.'

How to manage funding successfully

Operate short-term but think long-term

The limitations and frustrations of short-term funding can make longer-term strategic thinking feel impossible. However, to avoid crisis management it is important to develop a longer-term view, both of financial issues and of the longer-term strategic development of the organisation. A good business planning process should take the longer view, which will help the organisation to prepare a series of contingencies and possible longer-term plans.

Use the business plan

The business plan can be used as a valuable tool to explain the financial basis of the organisation, alert people to key risks, show that the organisation is thinking strategically and make the case for a sound organisational infrastructure.

Influence funders and involve fundraisers

Involving funders in the planning process can help them to understand the financial realities of the organisation and to find out the best ways their potential investment can be made.

As organisations grow there is a tendency to hive off fundraising and create a separate fundraising function. Fundraisers often see opportunities for future funding or feel that they would be more successful if the organisation developed in a particular way. This can lead to compartmental thinking or even conflicts between fundraisers and other staff. It is important that fundraisers are involved in the whole planning process and not simply given a target to meet at the end of the process. They need to understand the whole picture. Equally, the organisation needs to decide what it wants to do and then look for funding.

Exercise: testing your assumptions

This exercise is designed to test the assumptions upon which you are basing your plan.

There are three stages to the exercise:

1. Identify the assumption.
2. Test or challenge the assumption.
3. Decide what to do.

Stage 1: your assumptions

Under which assumptions are you planning? You might make assumptions about levels of support, the need for your services or the relevance of what you do, your role and the levels of resources available to you. Write each assumption as a short statement.

Stage 2: testing and challenging the assumptions

For each assumption consider the following questions:

What evidence do we have to support the assumption?

Which contrary factors challenge the assumption?

What could happen which might challenge this assumption?

How sound is this assumption?

Stage 3: deciding what to do

This stage is about deciding if you can carry on with the assumption or whether you need to take action.

Should we keep to the assumption?

If so, how do we keep it under review?

What action might we need to take?

✏ Exercise: managing new ideas and creating innovation

When did you last have a new idea? Many voluntary organisations pride themselves on being innovative. They see themselves as being dynamic and challenging, but what is the reality? Here is how one worker in a national organisation described her organisation's approach to new ideas.

If someone has an idea that they want to push for they have to be prepared to run an obstacle course of working groups, consultation meetings and discussion papers. It will take months. Any plan that emerges (and quite a few don't) will have had any inventive or creative element drained out of it.

Managing new ideas and creating innovation is testing for many organisations. This exercise aims to help you to evaluate the capacity of your organisation to be innovative and ensure that the plan does have a creative element.

List any new or dynamic ideas or initiatives that have got off the drawing board in your organisation in the past two years.

What are the factors that encourage innovation in the organisation?

What are the factors that discourage innovation in the organisation?

What does the organisation do to encourage new ideas? (Possible examples include having a research and development budget, evaluating current services, and encouraging project teams.)

How could this be improved?

What happens when new ideas or innovative projects go wrong?

What is the balance between ongoing work and new work in the plan?

How can new ideas, creative strategies and innovative work be encouraged in the planning process?

✎ Exercise: scenario planning

Many organisations, notably military organisations, use imaginary scenarios as learning and planning tools. The aim is to explore the future in order to become aware of what *could* happen and ultimately to be better prepared for what *will* happen.

Before you start the exercise, and with your chosen participants, discuss and decide its main focus and how far into the future you want to consider. The focal issue is best presented as a question. In the context of this chapter, it could be about the overall strategic direction, such as what challenges will our organisation face in ten years' time?, or about more specific questions, such as what will service users need or expect in five years' time?

To inform participants' thinking, it is useful to have already thought about which trends are likely to affect your organisation in the future. You can complete exercises such as 'predicting trends and developments' (see page 98) or a PESTLE analysis, where you consider the effects on your organisation of Political, Economic, Social, Technological, Legal and Environmental factors in the external environment. Keep in mind your chosen timeframe when carrying these out.

With this background, participants should:

1. brainstorm and describe possible scenarios that your organisation could face, keeping in mind the potential different trends and uncertainties identified in the preparation for the exercise;

2. think about and describe briefly how the organisation would be likely to respond to each scenario given the present level of preparedness (would it be chaotic, strategic, bureaucratic, coordinated, planned, hesitant, etc.?);

3. identify and decide on the most robust and effective strategic options, implications and actions;

4. identify early-warning signals for each scenario which can be monitored over time to help determine, over time, whether any given scenario is in the process of unfolding.

✏️ Exercise: ideas prompt worksheet

This worksheet is intended to encourage staff to identify ideas, options and opportunities for their area of work.

*Area of work:*_____

Are the original aims and ideas still valid?	*What has changed in this area since the last plan?*	*What are the likely key expectations and demands?*
Over the next three years what do you think will stay the same?	*Over the next three years what do you think will be different?*	*What are the main trends and developments?*
What is happening in the sector?	*What ideas are there for developing this work?*	*Which decisions need to be taken?*

Exercise: should we keep it going?

In the organisational analysis stage, activities or projects that are struggling or might no longer feel right for an organisation are occasionally identified. Some of the following factors might indicate a problem:

- The activity consistently underperforms. It struggles to meet performance targets. Uptake of its services is poor. It fails to deliver.
- The organisation can no longer get the support and resources to operate the project. Funders and commissioners are no longer interested in it. The organisation has to subsidise it to a worrying extent.
- An activity does not deliver enough outcomes that are relevant to the organisation's mission. It does not fit with the rest of the organisation and its work no longer is aligned with the organisation's strategy.
- A project takes up a disproportionate amount of the organisation's time. The organisation spends a lot of time trying to manage it.

It is useful to analyse a troublesome project in a logical and objective way. Answering the following questions can help:

How does this activity/project fit with our vision and strategy?	
Are the problems it is experiencing a temporary problem or more fundamental?	
What would the implications of closing or withdrawing from it be?	
Can it stay as it is?	
Could we use the resources tied up in this activity/project in a more relevant way?	
What options do we have?	

Option 1	Option 2	Option 3	Option 4

Exercise: how clear is the direction?

This exercise is useful to attempt after the main strategic aims of the organisation have been agreed. If the answers are uncertain or vague then it may mean that the direction agreed is not decisive enough. If the strategic aims are successfully implemented...

What will be different about the organisation?

Will it:

☐ Be bigger or smaller?

☐ Do more or fewer things?

☐ Have the same or different service users?

☐ Be generalist or targeted?

☐ Work in the same or different ways?

What will the key differences be if this strategy is implemented?

Try to describe the significant changes of the new direction as if you were writing a newspaper headline.

What will still be the same?

What will the organisation do more and less of?

More of:	Less of:

✎ Exercise: strategy planner

Strategic goal	

Intended outcomes

Key measures

Activities and outputs needed to obtain the outcomes

Outline work plan	*Costings and resources*	*Review*

Using the planner

Strategic goal

- Describe the intent.

Intended outcomes

- Describe the intended result.
- How will you measure success?
- What do you want to change or prevent?

Key measures

- How will you measure performance?
- How will you measure results?
- What will be delivered or produced under this goal (i.e. what are the intended outcomes and outputs)?

- Which activities and outputs are needed to obtain the desired outcomes?

Outline work plan

- Set out the work to be carried out.
- Outline costs.

Costings and resources

- What are the full costs involved in this activity?
- What staff time is needed?

Review

- What are the key milestones?
- When will progress be reviewed?

Chapter eight
Resourcing the plan

Once the strategic direction has been agreed, the in-depth planning work can begin. The detail about how the organisation will (or can) attract or earn the funds to do what it wants to do and deliver the strategy needs to be explored. All of the organisation's resources (people, money and materials) must be managed to ensure that they are being used to deliver the strategy or support the activities that fit with the organisation's strategic focus and support the delivery process.

This chapter looks at:

- the financial information needed in a business plan;
- forecasting income;
- establishing the break-even point and the break point;
- establishing what an activity costs;
- forecasting cash flow;
- some key financial questions;
- creating a business model of how the organisation expects to operate and to show how the organisation's resources will deliver the strategy.

The financial information needed in a business plan

There has been a tendency in recent years, particularly from banks and some larger funding bodies, to ask for business plans to project income for the next three years, give a detailed cash-flow analysis and show that the organisation is (and will remain in years to come) a safe and viable concern. This is often a pointless exercise. Few organisations in any sector can accurately predict their financial position much beyond the next financial year. However, financial information does play an essential part in a business plan.

To show potential investors the assumptions behind the plan, you need to demonstrate that the financial plan has been considered properly. This doesn't entail checking every item of anticipated income and expenditure line by line. However, the plan needs to show that the organisation:

- is financially viable and has thought through its financial policy and likely income and expenditure in an intelligent and realistic way;
- has made sensible assumptions about its likely financial future;
- has realistically and fully costed its activities and taken into account the need for contingencies;

- has sufficient financial controls to manage and plan properly;
- has coherent financial management policies.

In addition, you need to give careful consideration to how much financial information to include. Nowadays there is a high level of public scrutiny of voluntary organisations which requires them to be open and transparent about how they use their funds and resources. However, there is an interesting balance to be struck between being open and transparent for the public and not giving away valuable information. With this in mind, how you present financial information will depend upon two factors:

1. How open you wish to be about your organisation's financial affairs. For example, some organisations negotiating contracts have felt in a weaker position because their potential purchasers have had full details of their financial arrangements.

2. Your ability to be accurate about future financial projections. The further ahead you plan, the less certain your financial projections will be. One organisation produced draft income and expenditure forecasts on the following basis:

Year one: Monthly projections.

Year two: Quarterly estimates.

Year three: A rough estimate of income and expenditure for the year.

Changing role of finance: same job, different role

As voluntary organisations grow and develop, their financial processes and information need to change. In the past all that really mattered was ensuring that sufficient funding was obtained to cover planned expenditure. The emphasis was on the bottom line. Today's tougher funding climate, however, means that many organisations are facing difficult financial choices.

As a result of this, the finance role in many organisations is developing and changing and plays a key part in informing the strategic and business planning process.

Past: control and transactions	Future: finance as part of strategic management
- Ensuring proper financial control - Processing data and transactions - Managing information - Ensuring compliance - Controlling spending	- Linking financial resources to strategic priorities - Spotting trends and interpreting information - Helping to cost ideas and develop business models - Bringing some business sense or discipline to the process

One finance manager commented:

In the past I was treated as an overpaid bookkeeper. I spent most of my time saying 'no' because we could not afford to do something or because it wasn't in the budget. My role has become more strategic. It's now more about saying how we can do something and explaining the business and financial implications of a new strategy. Obviously the control and stewardship roles are still needed, but it is important that I am fully involved in putting the strategy together and not just in 'doing the numbers'. In the past we planned once a year when we put together the budget. Now planning is an almost continual process. The budget is not as fixed as it used to be. It has to be reworked throughout the year.

Forecasting income

An essential activity in financial planning for a business plan is to try to predict income trends in future years. However, many organisations are plagued by the short-term outlook of some funders and become caught up in an April-to-April scramble for cash.

The process of analysing income sources is often called a 'sensitivity analysis' (in the jargon of business planning). This should consist of three elements:

1. Reviewing the current position. How stable has income been in the past?

2. How you expect each source of income to develop. What is likely to happen to it? What is it dependent on? How reliable will it be?

3. The action needed to achieve the target. What can you do to secure this income? How can you protect or extend it through better marketing or better negotiating?

Possible income sources

- Grant aid from statutory bodies
- Service agreements and contracts
- Grants from trusts and companies
- Public fundraising
- Sponsorship
- Legacies
- Subscriptions and donations from members
- Profit from trading operations
- Earned income from the sale of services
- Hire of resources
- Investment income
- Management fees
- Consultancy fees
- Income from service users (such as rent)

Case study: predicting trends in current income

A community arts agency produced the following prediction of its likely sources of income for the next three years.

Income source	Current position	Predictions	Action needed
Grant from District Council for leisure and arts community development work	● 30% of income. ● Annually agreed. ● Use not specified.	● Will evolve into service agreement. ● Will probably stay at same level plus inflation.	● Push for three-year agreement. ● Sort out negotiating strategy.
Regional Arts funding	● 25% of income. ● Annually agreed.	● Review of arts funding strategy could have potential implications for us.	● Investigate review. ● Monitor the changing funding criteria.
Commercial sponsorship for artist-in-residence	● 14% of income. ● Will end this year.	● We could lose a management fee of £2,000.	● Look for alternative sponsorship.
Fee earned for local estate work	● 12% of income from four contracts.	● Difficult to predict. ● Do these projects cost us more than we think?	● Do marketing outside current area.
Hire of building for events	● 9% of income.	● Bookings will likely be down from previous years.	● Review, market and develop pricing plan.
Office space rented to outside group	● 6% of income.	● Due to increased competition it might be difficult to maintain this level of income.	● Schedule rent review.
Donations and miscellaneous income	● 4% of income.	● Will probably stay at this level of income with minimal effort.	● Consider if we need to review our fundraising strategy.

This activity quickly identified some issues for the management team members to address:

● Do we really know what each activity costs?

● Did we properly predict the full cost of each project or activity before we took it on?

One interesting aspect of this exercise was confirming that no individual in the agency had responsibility for managing specific income. Hire of the building, office rent, donations and sponsorship were all organised on an ad hoc basis. No one thought about them in a strategic way, but they accounted for 33% of the agency's income.

Establishing the break-even point and break point

In any venture the break-even point and the break point are of critical concern. The break-even point is the point at which income starts to overtake the fixed and variable costs of the operation; i.e. the point at which you start making a profit or surplus.

Break-even analysis has always had relevance when a service receives income for every time it gets used. Sometimes the break-even and break points are obvious and easy to identify and plan for; for example, a hostel needs to fill so many beds each night to remain viable. In other instances, however, it is less obvious how to identify when they might occur. For instance, the number of projects that an organisation can manage effectively or the number of active cases a worker can deal with may vary and is often learnt through experience and analysis of past work.

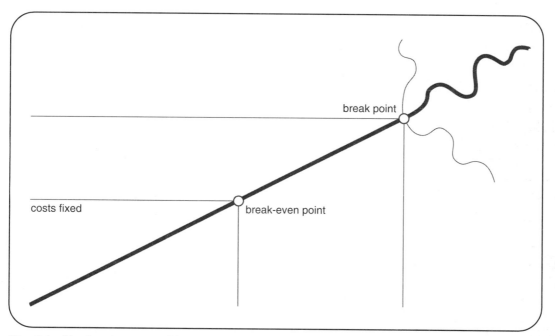

Fig. 8.1 The break-even and break points

The break point is that point at which the service reaches capacity. New clients can only be dealt with if extra resources (human and physical) are provided. Every organisation has a point where it becomes viable and certainly a point at which, if it continues to take on more work, it will have gone past its capacity. Beyond the break point it will then start simply responding to and managing crises. It is worth noting that sometimes the most relevant break points are not to do with cash income. They could include staffing levels, casework systems and physical space.

Case study: the community café's break-even and break points

The members of a team running a community café calculated that they would have to meet a fixed cost of £85 each week even if the café sold no meals at all. The fixed costs included rent, wages and payments on hire purchase (see the table below). The variable cost – the additional cost of every meal sold at £0.75 – was £0.40 for every meal made.

The team also calculated that at 244 meals the café would reach the break-even point, where income from sales would overtake the combined fixed and variable costs. At 244 meals the café would move into profit, the fixed cost would remain the same and only the variable cost of each extra meal sold would be added to the total cost.

However, they realised that a point would be reached when the growth of the operation meant that its ability to respond to growth would become inadequate. They estimated that at around 400 to 450 meals, the café would start to hit break point. It would need to invest in more equipment, more space and more staff to cope with increased customer demand. If it failed to do this, it would be likely that the service would start to suffer. The quality of both the food and the service would be reduced, staff could become stressed and customers might stop coming. The café could be harmed by its own success.

At the break point or, even better, well before the break point, the café would need to have the cash to expand its capacity to do business. This would add to its fixed costs (taking them to £170 per week) and, in the example shown, would take the café (hopefully only temporarily) back into a loss. It could plan for this by setting aside a certain sum each week to cover such expansion and increased cost.

Fixed costs: £85 per week

Variable costs: £0.40 (i.e. cost per meal)

Price: £0.75

Meals sold per week	Fixed cost £	Unit cost £	Total cost £	Income £	Profit/loss £
450	170	180	350	337.50	−12.50
400	85	160	245	300	55
350	85	140	225	262.50	37.50
250	85	100	185	187.50	2.50
244	85	97.60	182.60	183	0.40
200	85	80	165	150	−15
100	85	40	125	75	−50
0	85	0	85	0	−85

There are several important strategic issues to consider when discussing break-even and break points. Many voluntary organisations have a culture that encourages people to go beyond the break point, never say 'no' and somehow manage to provide a service to more people with either the same or declining resources. The long-term consequence of this is that a service becomes led only by demand, it only reacts to pressure and sooner or later the quality of work suffers.

The problem of the break point is a problem of success. Demand for the service has outstripped the capacity to supply it. The cause of small business failures frequently points to growing too fast or growing beyond capacity. In many instances managing rapid growth and increasing demand is as hard as managing crisis and decline.

In a profit-making enterprise it should be possible to see the break point approaching, produce a business plan that shows the venture's success and gain the financial backing to obtain extra financial resources to take it over the break point. When a voluntary organisation reaches a break point it is highly unusual for a funding body to offer additional cash because the organisation is very busy. Agreements between voluntary and statutory agencies are often very clear about the minimum service requirements, but are silent about the point at which the service being purchased reaches break point and a further contract, were a break point to happen, would have to be negotiated.

A voluntary organisation, then, would need to think through how it would react when it gets to a break point. Does it have a strategy for expanding to meet demand? How would it win support from funders and commissioners to do this? Or would it need to manage expectations and take action to cope with excessive demand by identifying its current capacity and managing demand in a fair and equitable way? The crucial thing is to think about the break point before you get to it.

Establishing what an activity costs

Beyond budgets

All organisations have some kind of budget. Traditionally, budgeting in voluntary organisations has been about making sure that there will be sufficient income to meet projected expenditure. The focus is on getting the bottom line to balance.

Changes in funding arrangements, the increased use of specific projects within organisations and an increased unwillingness to pay for core or administrative costs has led many organisations to move away from a traditional budget to one which more accurately shows the full cost of a specific activity.

A budget should be based on an organisation's key priorities expressed in financial terms. It commits an organisation's financial resources and sets targets for generating income. Once adopted, it becomes a control mechanism for keeping the organisation on track and ensuring that financial performance is as planned.

The way organisations use their resources is obviously a critical strategic issue, yet the approach to budgeting is often divorced from the way in which strategies are developed and implemented. The way the budgeting process is managed can make financial strategising difficult. Producing the budget is seen as an annual administrative duty and is delegated to the treasurer or finance staff. There are several problems with a traditional budget and budgeting process:

- **It's based on the past:** usually, the starting point for drawing up the budget is to look at the previous year's budget. The same format is used and the amounts are updated. The budget is based on what the organisation did in the past, not on what it wants to do in the future.

- **It can be inflexible:** once something is in the budget it is hard to get it out. The budget is agreed at the start of the year and it is assumed that it will be stuck to. Unforeseen events and new opportunities have to wait for the next budget.

- **It works against teamwork:** managers see *their* bit of the budget as something that they have to protect from other managers. It can encourage turf wars as managers try to build up their budget at the expense of others.

- **It encourages people to spend:** once something is in the budget it gets spent regardless. Towards the end of the budget year managers rush to spend any unspent budget, as an underspend might be seen as poor performance or a weakness.

- **It does not provide useful information:** the headings used to structure the budget do not relate to the organisation's work. It is often hard to identify what a project or service fully costs, as some key cost elements are hidden away or the indirect costs of managing and supporting the project are not properly allocated.

- **It is short-sighted:** the budget is usually for twelve months only, and so people argue that there is little point in planning beyond a year. However, the organisation's programmes, projects and commitments will probably run beyond a year, so people should not be discouraged from thinking beyond the end of the budget.

Here are some ideas to change and challenge the budgeting process:

Agree the strategy first, then budget

As advised elsewhere in this book, it makes sense to agree the overall strategic direction before starting the budgeting process so that budget decisions are informed by the organisation's strategic priorities and direction. In principle, every item of expenditure should be able to be justified by showing how it advances or supports the organisation's strategy.

Spot options

In most organisations, putting the budget together can seem like a set of foregone conclusions. Many major items of expenditure, such as salaries and building costs, are ongoing contractual commitments and are hard to get out of. A key skill of a strategic finance manager is to identify flexibility in the budget and spot possible options in the budget planning process. This will usually also involve identifying the process for and possible cost implications of reducing or getting out of some ongoing commitments.

Start from scratch

One radical approach that can challenge the historical base of most budgets is that of zero-based budgeting. This approach involves budget holders having to justify why each area of proposed expenditure should be included in the budget. 'It was in last year' is not a good enough reason to put it into next year's budget. Managers must show how each budget line fits with the organisation's strategy and will contribute to desired results. The process can reduce wastage and encourage a questioning attitude.

See budgeting as a continual process

You must challenge the idea that before the financial year an organisation can be confident that it knows almost exactly how much income it is likely to generate and what everything is going to cost. The budget should be reviewed regularly throughout the year to ensure that it keeps pace with developments and factors that could not be predicted at the start of the process.

Carry out full costing

A key development in voluntary sector finance is the recognition of the importance of working out the full cost of a project or service. This process (discussed in greater detail in the following section on cost centring) involves: 1) working out the full cost of an activity including what it costs the organisation to support and manage it and 2) including a contribution to the organisation's indirect or overhead costs. All too often organisations under-cost their work or (often due to pressure from funders) they try to hide away necessary management and admin costs. Fully costing activities gives much better management information as it enables managers to relate the cost of an activity to its value in terms of contributing to the organisation's strategic priorities.

Budget format

A traditional budget usually has the following format:

Income		Expenditure	
Council grant	. . . .	Salaries	. . . .
Trust and company donations	. . . .	Administration	. . . .
Fundraising	. . . .	Building	. . . .
Sales income	. . . .	Projects expenditure	. . . .
TOTAL		TOTAL	

Cost centring: what activities cost to operate

The traditional form of budget outlined above does not indicate what each activity or service costs. An alternative method of budgeting which charges expenditure to a particular activity or project is called cost centring or activity-based budgeting. Statutory bodies used to give grants to support voluntary organisations' work, but nowadays they are more likely to agree contracts to deliver services. Contracting is about purchasing a specific service from an organisation at a predetermined price. If the price is wrong, the service still has to be delivered. Contracts and service agreements, therefore, require an organisation to cost and price individual projects and services accurately.

A major development in this field is the emergence of the concept of full cost recovery. The publication of the first edition of *Funding our Future* (Brookes 2002) by the Association of Chief Executives of Voluntary Organisations (ACEVO) sets out a model for organisations to use to cost their work completely. *Funding our Future*, and ACEVO's later publications *Full Cost Recovery* and *Full Cost Business Planner*, make it clear that organisations cannot simply hide away or ignore their core management and administrative costs. At the same time, the Treasury commented that:

> *Funders should recognise that it is legitimate for providers to include the relevant elements of overheads in their cost estimates before providing a given service under service agreement or contract.*

HM Treasury 2002

Case study: working out the full costs

The Community Health Team is a voluntary project set up to help people adopt a healthier lifestyle and increase well-being. The team does this through information, providing advice and carrying out public campaigns. The team currently has eight main activities:

- An education programme: courses for teachers and health workers
- A Good Health week: an annual health promotion week
- A rural project: outreach work with isolated communities
- A resource centre: a library of materials for teachers to use
- An HIV/AIDS project: awareness work on HIV/AIDS issues
- A youth project: work with 16- to 22-year-olds
- Public enquiries work: telephone enquiry point
- Advocacy/development work: support for local health partnerships and initiatives

Its current budget is as follows:

Income	£	Expenditure	£
NHS contract	117,000	Salaries	124,000
Charitable trust grant for youth work	20,000	Admin costs	13,000
Project grant for work on HIV/ AIDS	14,000	Resources	4,000
Income from courses	16,000	Minibus	3,000
Income from sale and hire of resources	3,000	Good Health	7,000
Council grant for Good Health Week	4,000	Telephone	6,000
		Building costs	17,000
Total	174,000	*Total*	174,000

The project's staffing is:

	£
Manager	28,000
Education Officer	23,000
Information Officer	22,000
Field Officer	22,000
Resources Officer	19,000
Admin worker (part time)	10,000
Total	124,000

The budget had existed in this format for several years. However, the board decided to move to a different format that showed the full costs. The following reasons prompted this move:

- The budget did not show the full cost of individual activities or projects.
- Funders and purchasers wanted to know exactly what activities cost.
- The project needed to provide better information for bids and contract negotiation.
- The project found it hard to raise money for core costs or policy work.

After some discussion the project agreed to divide the team's work into seven project or programme areas:

- Education work
- Resource centre/information work
- Youth project
- HIV/AIDS work
- Rural project
- Good Health Week
- Policy development work

The first task was to divide all expenditure into three categories.

1. **Direct project costs:** expenditure directly linked to delivering services or costs incurred in supporting the delivery of services.
2. **Indirect costs:** central functions (administration, finance and personnel) plus the cost of governing the organisation and of organisational development.

To establish the direct staffing costs, each staff member divided up their time and put broad percentages against each of the cost centres. Using an activity log, team members allocated their time as follows:

	Manager	Education Officer	Information Officer	Field Officer	Resources Officer	Admin Worker	Total
Education	10% 2,800	70% 16,100			10% 1,900	10% 1,000	21,800
Resource centre/ information	5% 1,400	15% 3,450	70% 15,400	5% 1,100	80% 15,200	20% 2,000	38,550
Youth project	5% 1,400			20% 4,400		5% 500	6,300
HIV/AIDS	20% 5,600	10% 2300	10% 2,200	5% 1,100	5% 950	5% 500	12,650
Rural project	10% 2,800		10% 2,200	60% 13,200		5% 500	18,700
Good Health	10% 2,800	5% 1150	5% 1,150	10% 2,200		5% 500	7,750
Policy	20% 5,600		5% 1,150			5% 500	7,200
Non-allocated overheads/ indirect costs	20% 5,600				5% 950	45% 4,500	11,050
Total	28,000	23,000	22,000	22,000	19,000	10,000	124,000

The next stage was to allocate the non-salary expenditure.

	Admin £	Resources £	Minibus £	Good health £	Phones £	Building costs £	Total allocation £
Education	1,500	3,400	150			3,000	8,050
Resource/info	2,000		200		2,500	4,000	8,700
Youth project	500	300	800			3,000	4,600
HIV/AIDS	500	200	50			2,000	2,750
Rural project	600		750			2,000	3,350
Good Health	500	100	200	7,000		400	8,200
Policy	400		50			2,000	2,450
Non-allocated overheads/ indirect costs	7,000		800		3,500	600	11,900
	13,000	4,000	3,000	7,000	6,000	17,000	50,000

At this stage, the direct costs had been allocated. The elements that could not be allocated as direct expenditure represented the project's indirect or overhead costs, i.e. work involved in running the organisation and not delivering the service to users and communities.

	Direct staff costs £	Non-salary direct costs £	Total £
Education	21,800	8,050	29,850
Resource/info	38,550	8,700	47,250
Youth project	6,300	4,600	10,900
HIV/AIDS	12,650	2,750	15,040
Rural project	18,700	3,350	22,050
Good Health	7,750	8,200	15,950
Policy	7,200	2,450	9,650
Overheads allocated	*11,050*	*11,900*	*22,950*
Total	124,000	50,000	174,000

The final stage was to share out the overhead costs (i.e. expenditure that could not be allocated as a direct cost) amongst the seven projects. The total overhead cost was £22,950. The board decided that the simplest way to do this was that each project would take a share of the overhead costs.

The final allocation:

Cost centre	Direct cost	Add overhead share	Final full cost
Education	28,450	3,278	33,128
Resource/info	48,650	3,278	50,528
Youth project	10,900	3,278	14,178
HIV/AIDS	15,050	3,278	18,679
Rural project	22,050	3,278	25,329
Good Health	15,950	3,278	19,229
Policy	9,650	3,278	12,929
Total			174,000

Direct and indirect costs

Central to cost centring is the division between direct and indirect costs. Direct costs are the costs that are only incurred as a direct result of running the particular activity. An organisation's decision to run education courses would involve the cost of trainers, room hire, course material and probably most of the education officer's time, and if it didn't run the education courses it would not incur these costs.

Indirect costs are the shared organisational costs. They are costs that are difficult to apportion to a specific project or activity. For example, in the case study above, a portion of the manager's time, some administration costs and some building charges are counted as indirect costs. Organisations are finding it increasingly hard to obtain separate funding for indirect costs.

In some organisations the issue of what is a reasonable amount to spend on indirect costs as opposed to direct ones has become a controversial one. A hostel manager complained that she had to add £62,000 to her annual costs to pay for her parent organisation's indirect costs. She doubted if she received anywhere near £62,000 worth of management and central services back in return. In other sectors the reduction of indirect central costs either through 'creative accounting' strategies or by 'downsizing', where central services and jobs are cut, has been pursued zealously. Perhaps a more useful approach is to look at how central services can add value to the core projects and activities of the organisation through giving direction, providing support and the delivery of efficient services.

Moving to a cost-centred budget involves the following steps:

1. Identify the cost centres to use. This could be related to income sources or to work functions such as particular projects, activities or geographic areas. The centres used should be clear and distinct areas.

2. Allocate expenditure that can be directly apportioned to each cost centre. This will include supplies, resources and people's time. This process could be carried out on the basis of past usage ('on average the rural project uses the minibus for a third of its available time'). The ACEVO full cost recovery model provides a useful template for this process.

3. Agree how the remaining expenditure (the things that cannot be easily allocated to a specific cost centre) should be dealt with. In the case study, a fixed formula was used to divide the indirect costs between centres. The indirect cost is a charge to the activity or project to cover the central management or infrastructure costs.

Developing a cost-centred approach raises several issues. Many voluntary organisations have been historically poor at adequately costing their work: the cost involved in operating and providing good management has not been properly identified and has been under-costed or even ignored. The cost of spending or using other people's money can be high, and so under-costing can easily lead to a long-term crisis of struggling to do good-quality work on the cheap.

Indeed, many organisations which have moved into using cost centres have realised that the real cost of an activity is often far more than the grant or contract income that they receive from a statutory authority. This can raise a policy issue: should a voluntary organisation subsidise work carried out for statutory bodies? It also may help negotiators to adopt a more assertive approach in future contract discussions. There may be occasions when an organisation makes a strategic decision to take on an activity at a price which is below its full cost and then has to cross-subsidise or fundraise to fill the gap. In the past, the lack of any real costing information has meant that organisations have often drifted into activities without any real sense of the financial implications.

A negative side-effect of cost centres is that they can create an unhelpful competitive tension within the organisation where people in one centre can start claiming that they are 'more profitable' than others. This needs careful management. Cost centres provide management information that can help with making priorities and attaching financial value to activities, but the value of an activity should be measured in more than financial terms. A less 'profitable' activity can be contributing massively to the organisation's mission and achieving crucial outcomes: ensuring that this is communicated can help deal with any competitive unease.

Case study: a tale of two cultures

In the space of two weeks, the director of a community project had two different discussions about her agency's financial policy.

The voluntary sector liaison officer at the local authority told her that 'concern was being expressed' within the authority that the project's recently published annual report had shown an 'operating surplus' of £7,000. The project had decided to build up a reserve fund equivalent to six weeks' operating costs to cover cash flow, develop new ideas and cover any contingency. The local authority took a dim view of this. Council money was supposed to be spent on local needs, not sit in a bank account. The possibility of 'clawing back' unspent money was mentioned.

A week later a manager from a potential corporate sponsor visited to assess a proposal the project had made. The manager concluded the review by drawing attention to the lack of any future financial strategy and that a 'well-managed organisation should be building up a significant reserve fund for longer-term investment'.

This case raises three issues.

- The need to educate some funders and purchasers about the importance of sensible financial management practice. The business plan can play a useful role in this: it can set out the need for a sensible contingency fund and explain how any reserves are earmarked for a specific purpose.

- The importance of managing the relationship with funders. City corporations spend heavily on 'investor relations' – a form of internal marketing to stakeholders. Could a marketing strategy avoid such frustrations?

- A business plan should set out and make the case for a sound financial policy. If an organisation has developed reasonable reserves it needs to explain the reasons for them in a positive and not defensive way in the plan.

Forecasting cash flow

Business planners are often inclined to be very enthusiastic about cash-flow forecasts as many organisations have learnt the hard lesson that an anticipated cash surplus can easily be blown away by budgeted income not arriving on time. Cash-flow forecasting is about ensuring that there will always be sufficient cash available to meet anticipated expenditure.

In reality it is very difficult to accurately predict exact income and expenditure patterns and cash inflows and outflows for more than 18 months ahead. However, a business plan needs to show that:

- the impact of cash flow on the organisation's financial health has been considered;
- cash flow will be managed;
- the organisation will have sufficient cash reserves to meet its needs;
- the organisation understands its patterns of cash flow including seasonal ups and downs.

In looking at a cash-flow forecast it is useful to consider the following questions.

- Are there any points at which we will not have sufficient cash to meet our outgoings?
- What is our minimum monthly operating cost?
- How much working capital do we need to pay for expansion and development?
- What could we do quickly to improve our cash-flow position in an emergency?

Managing cash flow

A business plan may indicate the steps taken to manage and improve cash flow. Tactics for managing cash flow might include:

- writing payment schedules (possibly with penalty clauses) into contracts;
- monitoring payment of fees and grants;
- tighter control of people who owe you money;
- faster invoicing;
- spreading out expenditure in instalments;
- delaying some expenditure;
- delaying payment of certain bills;
- better banking arrangements.

Example: cash-flow projection

	12 months	April	May	June	July	August	September	October	November	December	January	February	March
Opening cash balance:	500	500	21,130	14,920	14,740	7,640	1,190	-980	14,300	11,180	5,160	3,690	1,420
Income													
Council grant	30,000	15,000						15,000					
Arts Board	25,000	10,000						10,000			5,000		
Sponsorship	14,000			6,000					4,000			4,000	
Fee income	12,000	2,000					5,000			1,000			4,000
Building hire	9,000	900	700	500	300	100	300	500	1,000	1,700	1,400	800	800
Rent income	6,000	500	500	500	500	500	500	500	500	500	500	500	500
Donations/misc.	4,000	400	350	350	250	250	300	400	350	350	300	350	350
TOTAL INCOME	100,000												
Monthly income:		28,800	1,550	7,350	1,050	850	6,100	26,400	5,850	3,550	7,200	5,650	5,650
Expenditure													
Salaries	42,500	3,220	3,260	3,330	3,500	3,500	3,670	3,670	3,670	3,670	3,670	3,670	3,670
Building cost	13,000	1,100	1,000	1,200	1,000	1,000	1,000	1,000	1,600	1,100	1,000	1,000	1,000
Admin	18,750	2,000	1,600	1,500	1,500	1,400	1,500	1,500	1,600	1,600	1,550	2,000	1,000
Phones	3,000	750			750			750			750		
Festival	7,200			600	200	500	1,200	3,000	700	800	100	100	
Projects	7,750	700	1,300	500	800	300	500	500	500	800	1,000	350	500
Equipment	8,000	400	600	400	400	600	400	700	900	1,600	600	800	600
TOTAL EXPENDITURE	100,200												
Monthly expenditure:		8,170	7,760	7,530	8,150	7,300	8,270	11,120	8,970	9,570	8,670	7,920	6,770
CLOSING CASH BALANCE	300	21,130	14,920	14,740	7,640	1,190	-980	14,300	11,180	5,160	3,690	1,420	300

(opening balance + monthly income – monthly expenditure)

Key financial questions to consider

The following ten strategic financial questions are useful in appraising an organisation's financial arrangements and financial strategy as part of the business planning process.

Do we have sufficient working capital?

Working capital is calculated by subtracting current liabilities from current assets. On a balance sheet, this is usually called net current assets. Every organisation needs sufficient working capital to ensure that cash flow can be managed, to develop new projects and to cope with unexpected events. Many voluntary organisations live a hand-to-mouth existence where the slightest financial difficulty can cause problems, and many are not able to follow up opportunities due to a lack of working capital.

Do we know what it costs to operate?

In order for costing to be accurate and realistic, organisations must develop costing systems that identify the true cost of a specific activity or service. These systems should fully take into account both direct and indirect costs and provide regular information that will ensure proper cost control.

How do we price our work?

The cost of an activity should be based on rational facts. The price at which a service is offered is usually based on a tactical or marketing decision. There are three possible strategies for pricing work:

1. **Plus-cost.** The cost is marked up by a fixed percentage to create some surplus and possibly also to allow some room for negotiation with purchasers.

2. **Under-cost.** The fee agreed is below the actual cost and the organisation takes on a piece of work in the full knowledge that it will need to subsidise it. There may be occasions when an organisation does take on work under cost, but it needs to have very clear reasons for doing so. Possible reasons include: to attract future work; because the organisation's cash-flow difficulties demand cash at any cost; and because the organisation is so committed to the activity that it is prepared to invest its own money in it.

3. **The price is set by the market.** There is a going rate or an agreed rate for the activity set by the purchaser or by other organisations. The organisation needs to see if it can recover its costs (or even create a surplus) within the price that has already been set.

Can we control the patterns of cash flow?

Managing cash flow is important. Ensuring that future funding arrangements take cash flow into account, scheduling income and expenditure and agreeing payment schedules can all help to overcome potential cash-flow problems.

How much does it cost to use other people's money?

The resistance of some funders to contribute to indirect costs or overheads means that the true cost of operating is sometimes ignored and organisations take on projects where the income only meets the direct costs. Rather than ignoring or hiding the real full cost of the project, however, managers and trustees need to know the reality, so make sure that your projects are fully costed.

Is the balance between direct and indirect costs right?

Getting the right balance between project costs and organisational costs can be hard. Some organisations suffer from having an over-staffed and over-resourced centre and an under-resourced front line. What is a reasonable balance between the centre and the projects? Is the centre too large for the current level of project activity? Does it add value to the project work?

Are we managing our income as well as our expenditure?

Most organisations have controls over their expenditure that stop them going over-budget. Is income also managed? Is sufficient attention paid to ensuring that income keeps to target, that shortfalls are picked up early, and that the future sources of income are carefully researched and managed? Is there any potential to charge for your services or to move into trading?

What sort of contingency fund do we need?

A contingency fund is an essential part of good financial management. Contingency funds cover unexpected cash-flow problems and unforeseen events and circumstances. There can sometimes be resistance to building one up, but the plan needs to show that the organisation has a credible approach to managing risk and a reasonable contingency fund is part of demonstrating this.

How will we replace capital items that depreciate over time?

Most capital items lose value over time. Each year the vehicles or equipment that the organisation owns reduce in value. On a balance sheet this is known as depreciation. The rate of depreciation depends on how long the item is expected to last; a proportion of the value is written off every year and some funds should be allocated to a fund to replace the asset at the end of its useful life. It is useful to check that there is sufficient money in the replacement fund to meet likely replacement costs and that the depreciation timetable is accurate. One computer training centre found out that their accountant had assumed that their computers would be replaced every ten years when it was likely that they would last for three years at the most. Money needs also to be set aside for repairs, refurbishment and decoration.

Do we have sufficient financial skills?

Do the in-house financial people (such as the treasurer and finance officer) have full control and are they able to provide regular and accurate monitoring information? Are the external financial advisers (such as the accountant and auditor) useful in financial planning and aware of tax, VAT and investment issues?

Ten costs often ignored

The following ten costs are often underestimated or simply ignored.

Start-up costs

These are the one-off costs involved with launching or establishing a project. Costs related to staff recruitment, moving in and launch publicity are often underestimated or create an early cash-flow problem.

Slow-start costs

Sometimes services start more slowly than anticipated. Organisations that sell their services or receive unit price contracts can experience below-target performance at what is often an expensive time due to the extra costs involved in the service's start-up.

Marketing costs

Costs for publicity, communication and image building are often ignored, which leads to poor or amateurish public relations and can cause credibility problems.

Working capital

Working capital is money which is not allocated or dedicated to a particular project or activity. It allows you to develop new projects and experiment. A lack of working capital means that new ideas and opportunities have to be ignored.

Research and development costs

Costs involved in service-user consultation, needs identification and service evaluation are often expensive and should be built into service budgets and plans to demonstrate good management practice.

Cash-flow costs

Many organisations operate to very tight cash-flow plans. A delayed payment from a funder or an unanticipated expense can easily knock a budget off course. Anticipating cash-flow problems and making necessary arrangements to survive a cash shortage can lead to extra costs.

Management and administrative costs

An extra project will usually demand additional management and administrative time and space from the main organisation. There is a danger of simply adding on projects and activities until the systems break down. Extra administration time, payroll costs and management time all need to be calculated. Volunteer management is another related cost.

Replacement and repair costs

Capital items such as computers, office equipment and other resources will usually need to be replaced at some stage. Many organisations have a replacement fund which accumulates cash for such costs. Is the contribution to the replacement fund sufficient?

Contingency costs

Staff maternity leave, sickness cover, legal costs and emergency repairs are all examples of contingency costs. Some organisations hold a central contingency fund to which all projects contribute. Some contingency costs can be met by insurance cover.

Close-down costs

There are often costs involved in closing down a fixed-term project that need to be built in. These could include evaluation costs, accounting charges, repairs and replacement costs of loaned equipment and buildings, and staff costs.

Business models

All organisations are based on some kind of model or framework that shows how money can be raised or earned and then used to fund the organisation's work. However, the model is often implicit or not described in any detail. A business model shows explicitly the key factors needed to make the organisation and the business plan work and how the organisation intends to fund itself.

In a purely commercial sense, a business model sets out how a business expects to develop, sell and distribute its services and also who it expects to buy them and how.

In a broader sense, a business model should:

- demonstrate what an organisation will do: how it will create or deliver value, organise and fund itself;
- show the thinking behind the organisation; outlining this can help you to challenge the assumptions behind it: are the assumptions about levels of demand and support and the organisation's likely role robust?
- demonstrate that the organisation is viable;
- illustrate how the organisation operates and fits together;
- show the interdependence of different elements, setting out how different activities and income streams relate to each other;
- identify the key business, financial and organisational risks involved; for example the withdrawal of one relatively small funding source could have a serious effect throughout the system;
- enable and encourage 'what if' questions such as what happens if business is much slower in the first year or what happens if particular costs rise? A good business model cannot accurately predict how the business will perform, but it does help people to understand it and what needs to be done to achieve success.

Some business models are incredibly simple but, as organisations grow, the models become more complex. Given the potential complexity, it is important that the model is understood.

The Business Model Canvas

Developed by 470 practitioners from 45 countries, the Business Model Canvas was created to provide a concept that everyone could understand, with the aim of helping people describe, discuss and analyse a business model. The creators believe that a business model is best described through the nine basic building blocks that the Canvas illustrates. (See 'References' on page 233 for details of the publication or www.businessmodelgeneration.com for further information.)

Figure 8.2 reproduces the headings from the Canvas and adapts for the voluntary sector the descriptions and questions the authors provide. Figure 8.3 provides a worked example of a community arts centre's Business Model Canvas. Given that there is no suitable equivalent term for 'customer' in the voluntary sector, this term remains in figures 8.2 and 8.3, and can stand for whichever relevant term is correct in any given situation, whether donor, supporter, beneficiary, volunteer or otherwise.

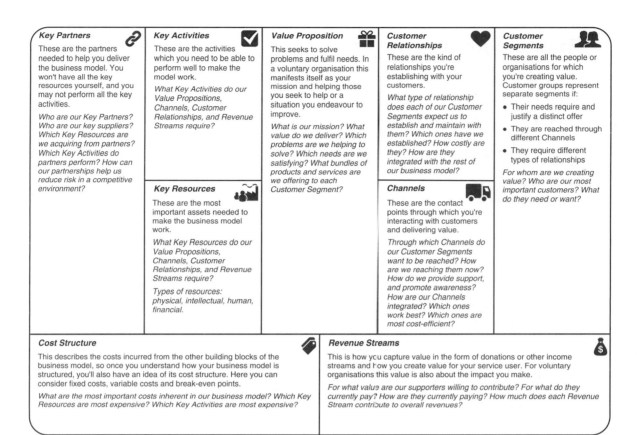

Fig. 8.2   Explaining the Business Model Canvas (businessmodelgeneration.com)

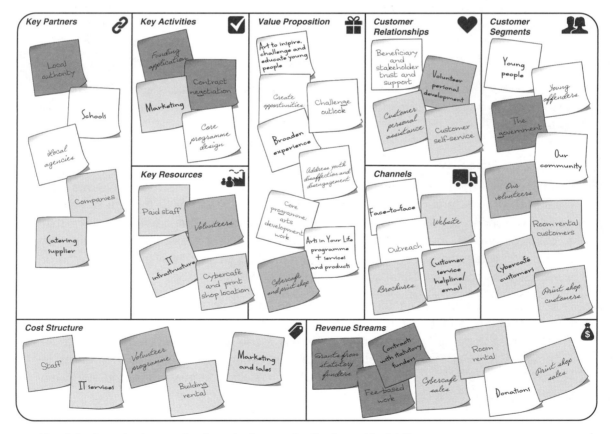

Fig. 8.3   A worked example of a voluntary sector Business Model Canvas

Adapted from Osterwalder and Pigneur 2010; this material is reproduced
with permission of John Wiley & Sons, Inc. and under the Creative Commons
Attribution-Share Alike 3.0 Unported License, businessmodelgeneration.com

The creators of the Canvas encourage:

- it to be used by a group of people and for ideas to be stuck on to it with sticky notes to keep the ideas moveable;
- starting the exercise again from scratch to sketch out alternative business models for the same activities;
- the use of both words and images to describe the business model's building blocks with the aim of helping people to understand the big picture;
- the use of colour coding to show the relationship between elements.

Developing the business model

Once the basic model is agreed, it can be developed to show the financial interrelationships between funding sources and projects. This helps to make clear the assumptions or risks involved. The model might rest on a basis that may no longer be the case over time; for example, it could be assumed that a charity will still be based at the parent charity's office and therefore enjoy cheap rent and the support of the charity's administration and office staff. However, if the business is projected to grow significantly will this remain a safe assumption?

The following case study develops the community arts centre's business model outlined in the Business Model Canvas.

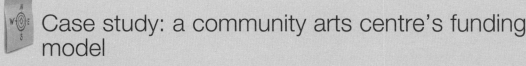

Case study: a community arts centre's funding model

The members of the community arts centre's planning group summarised their discussions on their chosen business model as follows, concentrating on the financial interrelationships between funding sources and projects:

- Grants and service agreements from public authorities are to pay the full cost of the centre's core programme of arts development work with young people. In the current year, income from public sector grants and service agreements was projected to comprise nearly 70% of the centre's income. The centre plans to work to create other income streams to reduce this proportion to about 55% in year 3 of the plan.
- All funding would include an element to pay for the centre's running costs and core staff team.
- The centre would develop a programme of 'Arts in your life' services and products that it could market to schools, local agencies and companies. The programme would be costed to include a contribution to the centre's management cost. This programme would be marketed on a project-by-project basis, but would be based on the skills and experience gained from the centre's core work.
- Through better use of its building the centre would develop and offer a set of rooms for rent, run a cybercafé and a small-scale print shop. These activities would generate income to use to develop new projects and reduce dependence on grant income.

Figure 8.4, overleaf, displays these financial interrelationships.

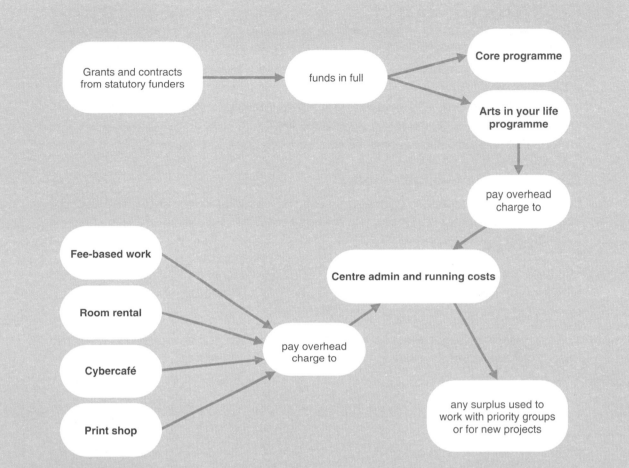

Fig. 8.4 A community arts centre's funding model

Highlighted issues

They went on to outline the assumptions and risks and the proposals to mitigate existing and anticipated problems by diversifying their model.

- An assumption that public sector funding was at best likely to stand still, but could decline. Over-reliance on it was a key risk. The centre needed a realistic strategy to bring in other income.

- For the centre to work, it needed a strong organisational core to provide administrative management and coordination, and to develop new projects. Although essential, obtaining direct funding for the core was proving to be hard to impossible. All future bids, projects and grant applications would need to include a full contribution to core costs.

- The centre has in its building a major asset that it was not currently using to its full potential. Offering space to rent and opening a café and print shop would increase the centre's use and bring in new income streams.

- The centre needed to encourage activities such as the café that might encourage new people to visit the centre and move on to other activities that the centre offered.

- The centre needed to develop a range of services and 'products' that it could offer to other agencies on a fee-earning basis. This might involve charging for some activities that, in the past, it had offered for free.

- The centre would need to become more commercially astute and develop some business and marketing skills, but not lose its core ethos and commitment to work with people who do not usually get involved in the arts.

Voluntary sector business models

Here are some variations of typical voluntary sector business models which can help you to consider the basic shape of your organisation's business model.

1. Win support/funding to do good work.

- Traditional charity model
- Simple to understand
- Well-established
- Attractive to growing or popular causes

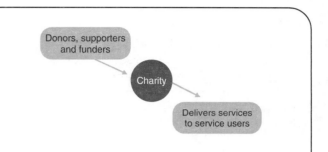

Description

A simple model. The organisation asks people and organisations to support its cause and donate money or give a grant. The organisation then uses the money to deliver services to the relevant beneficiaries.

Issues

This is a well-established and well-used model but it depends on the organisation's ability to present its case and convey to potential supporters the passion and conviction behind the cause. It can be difficult to sustain on a year-on-year basis. Donor fatigue can set in and it can lead to boom and bust where there is rapid growth when the cause or the organisation is popular and then decline as funders move on to other causes.

2. Core and projects model

- The organisation is a collection of projects
- Projects are supported by a core team
- Projects contribute to the core costs
- Projects are usually fixed-term

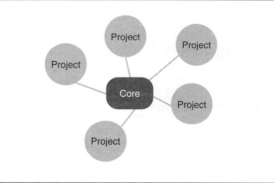

Description

The organisation develops funding or bids for contracts to deliver projects. Projects need a specific focus and can be organised around the location, type of work or type of service user. Projects need careful planning, as they are usually for a fixed term, so the organisation needs a strategy for how it can continue the work. The projects must also make a financial contribution to cover a share of the organisation's overheads or management costs.

Issues

This can be a complex model to organise because projects continually start and end. It is essential that the projects are fully costed to ensure that they cover their direct project cost and also contribute to the cost of managing and supporting the projects themselves. Some funders and commissioners have been reluctant to pay for full management and core costs. For the model to work, a strong core team is needed to support projects, connect projects together and plan how the work will be carried forward when and if the project ends.

3. Diversified/mixed income model

- A hybrid model
- Different types of income hold the organisation together
- Must be able to manage different relationships and working cultures: some work is grant-funded, other work commissioned and some might be paid for on a commercial basis

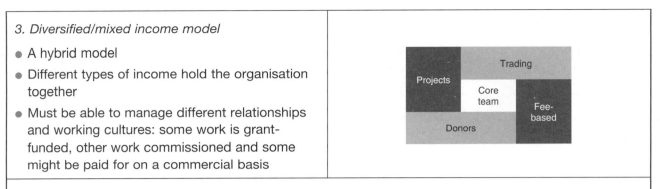

Description

The organisation seeks to avoid over-dependence on one or two funding streams by diversifying its income. Alongside traditional charity income from donors and supporters and managing projects, it generates income by operating some activities as trading ventures and charges a fee for some services to some service users. Profit from trading is used to support core activities or to fund new or hard-to-fund activities.

Issues

This model can give an organisation a level of independence and sustainability. It can raise ethical issues about how organisations should charge for services and to whom they should be charged. For it to operate it needs to develop key organisational and business skills and processes. It also needs to show how all activities fit with the vision, mission and values.

4. Loan finance

- Used to develop future revenue streams
- Seen as a possible alternative to grant funding for longer-term projects
- Loans must be paid back!

Description

In order to develop future services and new income streams the organisation takes out a loan, often with a specialist company. The loan is used to open new businesses or to win contracts. Loans are paid back at an agreed interest rate and to an agreed schedule.

Issue

Loan finance can be a way in which organisations can work on a bigger scale and create a more diversified organisation. Careful planning is needed to ensure that the organisation is confident and realistic that it will reach a point when loans can be paid back.

5. Franchise model

- A method for expansion
- An alternative to creating a single national body
- The licensing of knowledge, models and brands to others

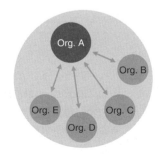

Description

An organisation expands by contracting with others to set up and run the service in their locality. The organisation supports and trains the other organisations in developing the service and lets them operate it as part of their successful brand in return for a fee.

Issues

This model works when an organisation has a successful and proven existing model or service that others might be interested in developing. The relationship is underpinned by a formal agreement to ensure consistency and protection of assets. There can be some tension within a franchised organisation about controlling the brand and ownership of the service.

6. Free and premium services

- Some services are offered for free or at a reduced rate to bring people in: a loss-leader
- A way of attracting people

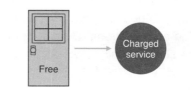

Description

The organisation runs some free activities because they get people through the door who may well then decide to purchase other services that are charged for at a rate that generates a profit.

Issues

When a service is sold at a loss to attract more business there is a danger that this can lead to more losses.

7. Prime and sub-contractor

- Development of a supply chain of prime or lead contractor and sub-contractors
- A business relationship
- Can be used to deliver large contracts

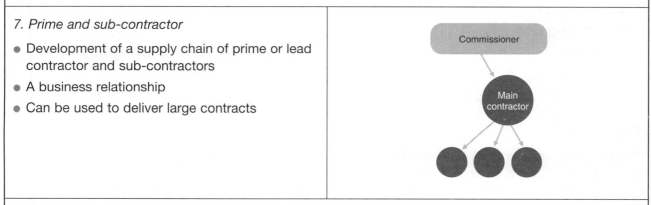

Description

An organisation bids for and wins a large contract. Rather than deliver it all itself, it appoints a range of approved sub-contractors to deliver elements of the main contract on its behalf.

Issues

Can be a way of managing large programmes, coping with capacity shortages and bringing in smaller or niche providers who would be unlikely to win the contract on their own. Needs to be underpinned by a clear agreement that sets out mutual expectations and how resources and risks will be allocated and managed. The main contractor remains responsible for the service even though elements of it are delivered by sub-contractors.

8. Working with others through a consortium

- A collaborative venture
- Stay independent but work together
- An alliance or joint venture

Description

Organisations with similar interests work together (possibly by creating and controlling a new venture) to create greater influence and make more of an impact (such as run a campaign or deliver a specialist service). The organisations retain their independence, but agree to collaborate and share expertise through the consortium.

Issues

Works best if there is a clear focus that unites the organisations. Needs an agreement that sets out a shared commitment, how it will operate and how work will be shared out. In the development of a consortium, a key challenge is to get members to see the bigger picture and see beyond the short-term interests of their organisation.

9. Outsourcing – the virtual organisation

- Contract out delivery
- Be flexible by relying on contracted and temporary staff
- Avoid fixed costs

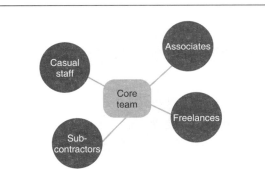

Description

Rather than employing people directly, the organisation delivers its work through a changing network of casual staff, specialist associates, freelances and sub-contractors who are hired or engaged as and when the work demands it. The organisation retains a small permanent core team to coordinate activities, win business and ensure quality.

Issues

This model can offer flexibility and the capacity to expand the organisation as and when work comes in. To be effective it needs a strong and stable core team to hold it all together and ensure consistency. It can be difficult to build up loyalty and commitment amongst a temporary workforce.

✎ Exercise: a financial health check

This exercise aims to help the planning process by focusing on three issues:

1. The recent financial management and performance of the organisation.
2. The importance of developing a coherent financial policy for the organisation.
3. The need to think about finance in a strategic, not a bureaucratic, way.

Think about the past few years and future possibilities and answer the following questions.

Financial history

How effective has the organisation been at costing projects? Have budgets usually been accurate or have certain costs been ignored or badly estimated?

How would you describe the pattern of cash flow in the organisation? Have there been regular peaks and troughs?

How have costs been allocated in the organisation? Have the core costs (such as management charges and administrative overheads) been recognised properly and shared out reasonably?

What has the balance sheet looked like? How strong has your liquidity ratio been?; i.e. how much cash (current assets) has been available to pay off current liabilities?

Financial management and systems

Do you have adequate systems of financial control within the organisation?

Do budget holders receive information which is up-to-date, relevant and accurately monitors planned income and expenditure in relation to actual performance?

Does the organisation's financial system give accurate information on what specific services and projects cost (including their contribution to the organisation's indirect costs)?

Are any particular costs volatile or highly variable? How will this affect the business plan? Can they be controlled better?

Are there sufficient financial skills within the organisation to:

• control income and expenditure?

- accurately cost projects?

- develop and project financial plans?

Do you anticipate any modifications to your budgeting or accounting systems? What improvements are needed?

Financial policy

Is sufficient income set aside for reserves and contingencies?

What proportion of the organisation's turnover would be reasonable to carry as a reserve or contingency fund?

Is sufficient income set aside to cover depreciation and for replacement costs?

Are the full costs of operating services and projects known?

Is the balance between central charges and direct costs of projects fair?

Financial projections

Over the next two years can you predict how income sources will develop?

Which income sources do you predict will increase?

Which income sources do you predict will decline?

What are your minimum operating costs in a month?

How flexible is your income? What proportion of your income is:

'earmarked' or committed for a particular expenditure?; i.e. its use is restricted:

dedicated from one year to another (for example salaries for permanent staff, contractual obligations to suppliers)?

Is there sufficient flexibility available to the organisation about how it uses its income?

Does current spending accurately reflect current priorities?

What costs could be reduced?
- direct project costs:

- indirect organisational overheads:

Financial strategies

Can you anticipate any significant changes in your organisational cost base over the next few years?

How effective is your charging or pricing policy?

Is there a coherent policy behind the charges that you make for your services to statutory purchasers, funders and consumers? What sort of pricing strategy do you currently use?

How does this compare with other organisations doing similar work?

How might this change?

Identifying a financial strategy

After reviewing your answers to the previous questions try to answer the following points:

What financial choices does the organisation have?

If the organisation were starting again what would be different about how it organised its finances?

What are the financial priorities for the organisation?

Exercise: predicting trends in current income

In column A, list all your current sources of income. In column B, note the proportion of your income this particular source currently represents. Also note any other relevant details, for example if the income is scheduled to end. In column C, describe what you currently know or predict is likely to happen to this income source (for example, will it get bigger or smaller or will the availability of it change?). In column D, note any action that you need to take to secure or better manage this income source.

After completing the columns, discuss how income can be diversified.

A. Income source	B. Current position	C. Prediction of trends	D. Action needed

✎ Exercise: a trading venture checklist

This list is a starting point for checking that the ideas behind a trading venture have been fully worked out. The checklist is not designed to determine whether or not to go ahead with a venture. Its purpose is to ensure that the key issues have been worked out properly and to identify areas for further consideration.

Strategic issues

1. Is the venture in line with our overall purpose and values? ☐
2. Does it fit with our organisation's strategy? ☐
3. What reaction might we get from users or funders? ☐

Business issues

4. Has the intended service or product been clearly defined? ☐
5. Have the legal and tax issues been properly considered? ☐
6. Has it been fully costed? ☐
7. What is the likely pattern of cash flow? ☐
8. How would start-up or slow-start costs be met? ☐
9. Are the potential risks involved reasonable? ☐

Organisational issues

10. Do we have the skills, systems and time for this venture? ☐
11. Are we sure that this venture will complement our main work? ☐
12. Is the level of organisational input into the venture worthwhile? ☐

Chapter nine
Establishing credibility

A business plan needs to make the case for why an organisation should receive support. It must establish confidence in the minds of potential backers that the organisation is competent enough to manage the plan successfully. For smaller organisations or newer projects the plan can also help to show that there are sufficient support systems around the organisation to enable it to achieve its strategy.

Many voluntary organisations seem reluctant or unwilling to record or market their own expertise, skills and competence positively. The process of collecting this information can have some very useful effects, however, by putting organisations in a much stronger position with funders and purchasers and increasing their confidence. A manager of a trust that requires business plans as part of its application process commented:

> *The idea behind the plan may well be brilliant, but we need to know that it has the people and systems in place to implement it. We look to the business plan to convince us that the organisation has a good track record and that the key personnel involved are experienced in similar activities.*

This chapter covers how the business plan can demonstrate credibility by showing evidence that the organisation has:

- a history of doing good and effective work;
- systems, processes and structures in place that are appropriate to the scale and demands of the plan;
- a core of personnel within it with sufficient skills to implement the plan;
- in the case of new initiatives, carried out sufficient feasibility work on the plans;
- a strategy to achieve the plan;
- identified real and potential risks involved in the plan and has taken action to avoid them.

Evidence of your past achievements

The following points are possible sources of evidence to demonstrate that an organisation has a good track record.

External evaluations

Independent evaluations carried out by a researcher or expert can indicate the strengths of the organisation and show that it is committed to improving and learning from its work.

Feedback from service users

Positive feedback which has been recorded from service users and evidence of repeat work indicates that the organisation is capable of providing a service that people want and value.

Third-party references

Endorsements from eminent people in fields related to the organisation's specialist area can help establish credibility. A health group, for example, used evidence of support from medical consultants in its business plan to establish credibility with health purchasers.

A list of past clients

Displaying a list of current or past client organisations or partners can help establish credibility, particularly if any of these agreed to act as referees.

Evidence of successful work

Press cuttings, case studies and evidence of the difference that you have made to past clients can help to create a positive feel about the organisation.

Evidence of organisational competence

A business plan needs to show that the organisation has the necessary systems and processes in place to manage the plan properly. The following areas can help to provide some evidence.

Policies and procedures

The existence of an equal opportunities policy, a complaints procedure, some staff development policies and other statements might show that, on paper at least, the organisation is clear about how it should work.

Sound financial management

Previous accounts and audits can show that the organisation has managed its financial affairs properly in the past.

A quality assurance policy

Quality assurance is about finding out from service users what is important about how the service operates, establishing minimum quality standards that indicate what can be expected from a service and ensuring that the organisation consistently meets the standards.

A quality-assurance policy should set out key standards and indicate how they will be monitored and improved. The use of PQASSO (Practical Quality Assurance System for Small Organisations) developed by the Charities Evaluation Service is one way of showing that the organisation has reviewed itself against standards designed to encourage good organisational practice. (See www.ces-vol.org.uk/PQASSO for more information.)

External awards

In some industries the award of the International Organization for Standardization's quality management standard, the ISO9001 (the only standard within the ISO9000 family of standards that can be certified), is an almost mandatory requirement. Some contracts are only awarded to companies with ISO9001 accreditation. All that the ISO9000 family of standards demonstrates is that the management practices used to manage a system are rigorous and comprehensive enough to satisfy an external audit. It does not comment on the benefit to service users of the service being provided or the relevance of the standards set.

Another external accreditation is the Investors in People (IPP) standard which is awarded after an external review of an organisation's staff training and development policies. (See www.iso.org and www.investorsinpeople.co.uk for further information.)

Membership of a national organisation

Many smaller organisations or projects could point to their membership of a national organisation as evidence of having back-up services such as training, specialist advice and information. The national organisation might also provide some quality-assurance functions.

Audits and inspections

Evidence of successful external inspections can also be used to show that the organisation is well-managed.

Evidence of staff competence

Some business plans include the outline curriculum vitae of all the management team members. This may be going into too much detail, but to convince backers that the organisation has sufficiently skilled people within it, it is useful to provide:

- background details and experience of key staff;
- background details and experience of management committee and trustees;
- names of external advisers, accountants, solicitors and specialist consultants;
- relevant qualifications held by staff;
- staff development policies.

Case study: proving credibility

The Family in Crisis charity was set up by parents and some professionals to provide counselling, support and help to families in times of turmoil and stress. Initially the group worked with a network of volunteers coordinated by a worker paid for by a trust. However, changes in community care prompted the committee to approach local health commissioners to discuss how they might work together and the possibilities of financial support.

The first discussion with the commissioners was positive. The charity's services fitted in extremely well with several elements of the community care plan and with current priorities. The commissioners asked for a business plan so that they could consider it further.

The draft business plan followed a format set out in a high street bank's new business guide. The section asking them to 'list the relevant experience of key personnel' was initially difficult to complete. The health authority officers had commented that it was of concern to them that all 'potential providers were professional'. At first, this was seen by the committee as a weakness as they were 'only volunteers'. It seemed to them that the criteria favoured businesses or statutory organisations and put a small voluntary organisation at a disadvantage.

However, the committee carried out an exercise to identify and record the various skills they had. Amongst the committee's membership were a finance manager in a private company, a retired headteacher, a legal executive and a woman who had set up and now ran a successful small business. The group had within it significant management expertise, but perhaps as important was their combined local knowledge, contacts and personal experience of living with and surviving family crisis.

The charity also had a network of people around it who had provided help and support during different stages of the charity's history. They included two doctors, an assistant director of social services and a psychotherapist. These individuals agreed to form an advisory panel to the charity, separate from the management structure, that would advise the management committee and ensure a high-quality service.

Despite their initial doubts, it became clear that the charity had, within or around it, considerable skills and experience.

Proving that new activities are feasible

Many small businesses and voluntary-sector projects fail because the individuals who start them are so full of passion for their project that they don't think to carry out a genuine feasibility study. The commitment to the vision and dream becomes so important that questions such as 'will it work?' and 'who will pay for it?' are seen as negative and diversionary.

Ideas for new activities will have been explored during the developing options/setting the strategic direction stage (as outlined in Chapter 7). At this later stage, the thinking has been done and the decisions made. Now the business plan needs to prove that the project is viable by showing:

- how the need for the project has been identified;
- what the need is;
- how the proposed project will meet the need;
- the durability of the project and how it fits with the organisation's mission and values;
- the expected benefits;
- how the new project will fit within the organisation;
- what support there is for the project;
- that it has been fully costed, including start-up costs;
- how it has been researched and tested.

Evidence should be included to show that possible pitfalls and alternatives have been explored. A useful exercise to collect this evidence is to try to predict all of the potential questions and challenges there will be to the project and then assemble evidence to answer them. In discussing a project's feasibility it is also useful to identify in the business plan the potential risks in the project and suggest how these risks can best be managed. It is better to acknowledge a risk first and deal with it than to let someone else identify it as an undisclosed weakness (see also page 185).

Demonstrating how you will achieve the plan

The business plan needs to show that the organisation is capable of delivering the plan, i.e. it has the management and internal capacity to deal with the challenges required by the strategic direction set out in the plan. This is often called being 'fit for purpose' and includes managers anticipating and planning for the various internal changes that will be needed as a result of the plan.

Dealing with internal changes

In instances where an organisation has an ambitious strategy or one that takes it into new areas of work, the plan needs to show that the internal implications have been thought through and planned for. Possible areas in which there may be implications include:

- **Skills and expertise:** a different skill set from the one that the organisation currently has. It is useful to think through what new areas of expertise may be needed and to identify how they might be developed or brought into the organisation. For example, the managers of a community care agency recognised that in order to start selling some services to clients on personal budgets the organisation would need to develop some skills in business development, marketing and pricing work.

- **Legal implications:** a review of how the organisation is governed and the relevance of its governing document. All activities should fit within the aims, objects and boundaries (such as geographic) defined in the governing document. Governing documents can become dated so it might be necessary to update or amend parts of it to reflect the intended strategy.

- **Policies and practices:** the strategy might mean that the organisation has to develop new ways of working and hence changes to or new documented policies or procedures may be needed.

- **Role/job changes:** a full review of the kinds of roles that people play within the organisation to ensure that the roles are aligned to the organisation's new strategic direction. It could be that a new strategy changes the emphasis of a job, the kinds of roles that people play and the way in which performance in the job will be measured. It is important that the focus is on the job and not the individuals currently in that role. Managers need to give thought to how they can help and support people to recognise the differences in the role and in some cases it may be necessary to get good expert advice if, as a result of the strategy, a post has now become redundant.

- **Systems change:** some of the organisation's processes and systems need to be updated to support the new strategy. For example, an agency that intended to expand into new areas of work found that its information technology systems were out of date and would struggle to cope with any additional demands.

Case study: mind the gap

A voluntary organisation working with people with disabilities carried out this exercise to look at what it needed to do to be able to operate in a personalised care market where their service users either held their budgets or had much greater control or influence over them.

Current position → THE GAP → Intended position

Our services are funded by block contracts from social services. They tell us who to work for.

Service users contract with us directly for what they want. Service users become 'customers'. They choose what they want and pay us directly.

Gap analysis

The organisation identified seven key gaps and a change plan for each one.

Gap	Description	Change plan
Expertise	• Be more entrepreneurial, efficient and systematic about developing and selling services.	• Ask our trustees with commercial experience to mentor us in doing this.
Profile	• Find ways of marketing our services to potential service users.	• Produce service brochure and improve website.
Access/contacts	• Find ways to get to potential service users.	• Produce material for GPs, district nurses and other care workers to make it easy to refer people to us.
Capacity	• Create new roles to support a personalised care business.	• Develop new staff structure to create new post of Operations Manager to coordinate processes and customer care.
Skills	• Develop new skills and approaches in all staff that encourage flexibility and respect service-user choice. • Train staff to take on new roles.	• Develop key competencies. • Carry out a skills audit. • Implement individual training and development plans for all.
Organisational	• Adapt our IT and financial systems to be able to cope with lots of individual transactions.	• Appoint an external consultant to see if we can adapt our current system.
Internal	• Create a new way of working and culture with the aim of giving service users real power and choice. This could challenge some staff.	• Emphasise that we support service user choice. Managers to work with staff and teams on this.

Critical success factors

Critical success factors are the things that must be in place or due to happen if the organisation is to be successful in implementing its plan and ultimately achieving its mission. They are the internal ingredients that will be the cause of your success and therefore are the factors that the people leading the organisation need to ensure are developed and sustained. (The case study below outlines some examples of critical success factors.)

Critical success factors should be:

- **few in number:** ideally around three to eight; if there are many more, an organisation will lose its focus;
- **things that the organisation is capable of:** they should be a mix of realistic and challenging factors;
- **measurable:** managers should be able to quantify them;
- **capable of improvement:** managers should be able to develop them;
- **essential:** if a critical success factor is absent it is unlikely that the organisation will be successful.

Identifying critical success factors can help managers to focus on where they need to put their energy and effort. They need to be reviewed regularly to ensure that progress is acknowledged and the choice of factors remains relevant. It is also useful if responsibility for leading on a particular factor is clearly assigned to an individual – although the responsibility for it should be collective across the organisation.

There are four stages in developing critical success factors:

Stage	Issues
1. Identify what management action will be needed to deliver the plan.	• Work out what you need to do (or keep doing) to deliver the plan. • Ascertain the key management or organisational challenges posed by this strategy.
2. Create a list of possible critical success factors.	• Gather together everyone's ideas for possible factors.
3. Decide which ones to focus on.	• Agree which of these factors are *critically* important for the success of the strategy. • Don't take on too many.
4. Agree an action plan, allocating responsibility for it and for how it will be measured.	• Decide what you can do to improve or sustain performance for each factor. • Agree who has overall responsibility for each factor. • Choose what you will use to monitor and measure performance: i.e. the *effects* of the actions taken (as a result of your critical success factors). Key performance indicators are a useful way of measuring your organisation's results and impact (some examples are provided in the following case study).

Case study: developing critical success factors

A disability support service provides an information service, a telephone helpline and specialist casework for people referred to it. Its newly adopted business plan committed the organisation to an ambitious expansion plan in the hope that, by diversifying, the service would be more sustainable and less dependent on one main funder.

The plan had five main goals:

1. To continue to provide a responsive and high-quality service to clients that represents good value for money.
2. To develop a volunteer support service for carers after a successful pilot scheme.
3. To develop the potential of using social media to support and connect people.
4. To increase the hours that the volunteer-run helpline is open.
5. To develop a specialist service for families coping with complex issues after a successful pilot scheme.

The service's management team spent time looking at the management and organisational implications of these goals and drew up the following action plan to include in the main plan:

Critical success factor	Actions	Measures (key performance indicators)	Overall responsibility
Recruit and retain a sufficient number of volunteers	• Run regular campaigns to acknowledge the role of our volunteers • Create a dedicated volunteer development worker role	• The number of trained volunteers in place • The number of new volunteers recruited • The results of a volunteer satisfaction survey	• Director and HR manager
Use and develop IT systems	• Review all of our current systems • Establish IT 'local experts' to support colleagues	• Fewer system failures • The results of a volunteer satisfaction survey	• Operations Manager
Maintain and develop effective relationships with funders and commissioners	• Have regular meetings with key individuals so that they see their role as investors and partners • Develop and implement systems to record client feedback and progress so that we can collect evidence of our work • Involve funders in service planning	• The tracking of repeat funding rates • The development of specialist funding streams, such as for addictions work	• Director • Fundraising Manager
Maintain high-quality services that meet best practice	• Produce a simple quality standards framework • Develop a lead volunteer role to increase support to volunteers	• The results of a quality audit	• Operations Manager
Carry out effective marketing of all our services to new and existing partners	• Raise our profile • Obtain media coverage • Develop our brand identity	• The amount of media coverage • The level of contact with new funders	• Director

The service's Director commented on the process:

Doing the work on identifying the critical success factors was actually very useful. We knew most of them already, but it was helpful to spell them out and to focus on what we could do about them. We now regularly review them at management team and trustee meetings.

It is also useful to look at activities and projects that you regard as having been successful to see if they might be the source of critical success factors. It might be that what made a particular project successful could be replicated in other future projects and identified in the business plan as an organisational critical success factor.

Case study: identifying critical success factors by learning from the past

The staff, volunteers and board of the Ridley Youth Project used this tool to start the process of setting their critical success factors. They found it to be a useful exercise to help people understand how critical success factors work and therefore how to set future ones.

After some discussion, the team identified three successful episodes in the organisation's recent history.

	Episode 1	Episode 2	Episode 3
What was the occurrence?	• Organising and supporting young people to contribute to the council's consultation on the town's priorities.	• A 'drink safe' initiative to alert young people to the health dangers of binge drinking.	• The design, project management and refurbishment of a new centre in the middle of Ridley.
What happened and how was it successful?	• We developed our role as enablers and supporters of young people. • The event demanded significant preparation time. • We experimented with and developed our use of social media. • We worked with diverse groups of young people – not just the ones we knew.	• We developed strong partnerships with the NHS, the police and social services. • We created good relationships on the ground with other workers. • We tested the draft campaign material on young people before the launch. • We monitored and evaluated the project effectively to show what outcomes we delivered.	• Young people were involved in the centre's design throughout. • We had a clear project management process. • We asked a broad range of supporters for help. • We ensured that the project was fully costed and didn't do it on the cheap.

By reflecting on these three episodes, they were able to identify the critical success factors, useful behaviour and actions that helped to achieve them:

What were the critical factors that contributed to these successes?	• Engaging successfully with young people. • Collaborating effectively. • Creating clear objectives and goals.
How did the people responsible for them act?	• Each activity had a clear leader. • Leaders brought in other people: they facilitated the smooth running of the projects rather than trying do it all themselves. • They were willing to try new things.
How were they managed or planned?	• Using good, formal project management techniques. • An evaluation process was put in place with the involvement of stakeholders. • The project was fully costed.
What can we learn from them?	• To be creative. • That our strength/asset is our connection with young people and our ability to involve them. • That people want to work with us. • The importance of taking time to do formal planning and not rushing into things.
How can we use this experience in the future?	• To ensure that we build on our unique relationship with young people. • To ensure that we plan the delivery of all our projects to reflect best practice.

Showing that you have considered risk

All organisations encounter some kind of risk. In recent years, management thinking has encouraged people to be more methodical about risk: to identify possible risks, assess the chance of each risk happening and identify any necessary actions to manage and prevent the risk. The alternative is to avoid risks and try to crisis-manage them if and when they happen, which is not a wise option.

> *So let's get this clear – you run a hugely over-subscribed service to a diverse, demanding and challenging client group delivered by staff employed on a one-year contract and supported by volunteers who can walk away whenever they want. You operate in a marketplace and sector that is turbulent and changes fast. At the most your income is agreed for the next 12 months. Yet, you cannot see any point in talking about managing risk or future strategy!*
>
> Comments of a new trustee after her first management committee meeting

It is important to keep risk in perspective, however. One manager commented that the risks involved in his organisation were so great that he wondered why anyone stayed around!

At the stage in the process where the organisation has decided what it wants to do, it needs to consider the likely risks involved in order to show that the organisation has carried out due diligence. This involves reviewing the main risks that could threaten the organisation's ability to deliver the strategic plan. The business plan should show that managers have thought through the risks facing the organisation and have a series of plans in hand to prevent and manage them.

Identifying risks

A simple and useful exercise to identify the key potential risks facing the organisation is to cluster the risks into the following main groups:

- **Tangible or physical risk:** the more obvious risks such as a crisis caused by fire, flood or major event.
- **Service-delivery risks:** the risks involved in delivering the service to those using it, such as breaching a duty of care, bad or illegal practice or sub-standard service which leaves the organisation facing legal action.
- **Financial risks:** including accuracy and timeliness of financial information, inadequate reserves and poor cash flow, lack of diversity of income sources, poor investment management and the risk of fraud or of unknown costs.
- **Organisational risks:** internal factors such as employment issues, health and safety issues, and key staff or volunteers leaving.
- **Political and reputational risks:** including changes in government policy or demographics, and threats to an organisation's good name and standing; for instance a local branch gets bad publicity which affects the organisation as a whole.
- **Market and business risk:** any risks related to the external environment such as a change in demand or the entry of new forms of competition into the market.

There are other ways of grouping risks, such as governance, operational, environmental, etc. See *Charities and Risk Management* (Charity Commission 2010) for more information on this.

A simple risk-management framework is useful in discussing risk and identifying long- and short-term action. Each risk is assessed against:

- the likelihood of it happening;
- how much of an impact it would have on the organisation;
- any actions needed to prevent it;
- the contingency plans needed to manage it.

Case study: managing risk

The management board of a community regeneration agency identified six key risks that they needed to manage.

	The likelihood of it happening	The potential impact of it	Action needed to prevent it	Contingency plan
Risk 1: All our funding is short-term! Risk that all projects close in 18 to 24 months' time.	Medium: depends on our ability to secure new funds or extensions to existing funds.	• Critical issue.	• Start developing exit strategies for each project. • Have open discussions with funders.	• Must develop new projects.
Risk 2: We are dependent on a small team of volunteers – risk that some volunteers might leave.	Medium: numbers will fall if we do not retain or recruit volunteers.	• Important that we remain a volunteer-based agency – we do not want to be reliant on paid staff only.	• Increase volunteer recruitment. • Develop a volunteer retention plan.	• Run a volunteer recruitment campaign. • Develop a succession plan.
Risk 3: Cash-flow risk: some of our funders pay late or in arrears – we might not be able to pay our bills.	High: increasingly being paid late by the local authority.	• Threatens our financial security and ability to pay staff.	• Set up monthly cash-flow monitoring process. • Discuss with council.	• Set up loan facility. • Renegotiate payment schedule in service agreements.
Risk 4: Poor relationship with local authority – risk that councillors don't like us and could cut our core funding.	Unknown: hard to know what the council think of us.	• Increased concern about our relationship to the council.	• Talk to council officers and councillors to establish how they see us. • Invite them to visit us – renew relationships.	• Find new contacts in the council who will support and champion our work.
Risk 5: Risk that other agencies might move into this area and start winning contracts.	Medium.	• Depends if we cooperate or compete.	• Identify who might be moving in – is there a possibility of working together?	• Develop strategies on how we can work together and not compete. • Work out what we do best.
Risk 6: Our building is old, dilapidated and costly to maintain – risk of safety breach or higher maintenance and repair costs.	High: the state of the building continues to deteriorate. Needs action.	• Could be serious. • Risk of accident and a longer-term risk that the building gives off an entirely wrong image.	• Carry out health and safety inspection of building. • Draw up ideas and plans to improve the building. • Set up meeting to discuss our concerns with the landlord.	• Depends on response from landlord. • If negative, consider building move and set up capital fund.

Approaches to risk

- Be open about risks: they are inevitable.
- Develop early-warning systems for risks: what would indicate that you are moving closer to the risk becoming a reality?
- Ensure that each risk is managed: someone in the organisation should be named as being responsible for monitoring each risk, ensuring that preventative action is being taken and that the risk is regularly reviewed and reported on.
- Discuss the risk before you get to it: build consideration of risks into all project appraisals and new plans.
- Benchmark your risk management against others': find out how you manage specific risks compared to similar agencies.
- Learn from risks: when something goes wrong, consider why. What could you have done differently?

What to do once you have identified the risks

1. Accept the risk

Some risks go with the territory: they are a known feature of the sector and there is very little that can be done about them. Examples of this kind of risk in the voluntary sector include building an organisation delivering essential services that people depend on, using short-term funding only. Accepting the risk as 'normal' could be seen as being complacent and possibly not fully recognising the potential impact it could have on the organisation, but there are some circumstances where those evaluating risk in an organisation can feel comfortable about actively accepting a risk (such as taking on a fixed-term project) because they are used to it and can live with it.

2. Work to reduce the risk

Once identified, it might be possible to take preventative action to reduce the chance of a risk happening or to reduce its potential effect. Clear action plans to reduce risk include having better procedures in place, increased amounts of staff training and supervision, better-designed processes and the implementation of early-warning systems to flag up potential risks. It is unlikely that such actions will ever completely eliminate the risks; however, they might reduce the chance of their happening and show that the organisation has been diligent and serious in taking proactive steps to manage them.

3. Develop safety nets

One approach is to have clear plans in place to manage and react to any given risk if it were to happen. Such plans might include contingency arrangements, insurance and having a plan B in reserve. These arrangements need to be in place in advance of the risk happening. The plan needs to show how the safety net can be implemented. Management should check regularly to ensure that the plan is up to date and contains effective responses to anticipated problems.

4. Pass the risk on

It might be possible to identify another agency or agencies which are better equipped, skilled or prepared to manage the risk than you are.

5. Withdraw from the risk

In some instances it might be appropriate to decide that, in order to protect the organisation's future and reputation, you need to withdraw from the risk and reduce your exposure to it.

Exercise: proving your track record

A business plan should show that the organisation is capable of achieving its plan. It will need to show evidence that the organisation or the key people within it have the competence and experience to manage the plan successfully.

What evidence do you have of the following elements?

External evaluations

Feedback from service users

Third-party references

A list of past clients/partners

Policies and procedures

Sound financial management

Quality assurance

External awards

Audits and inspections

Staff competence

Critical success factors

Identified risks and responses

What other strengths or organisational assets need highlighting in the plan?

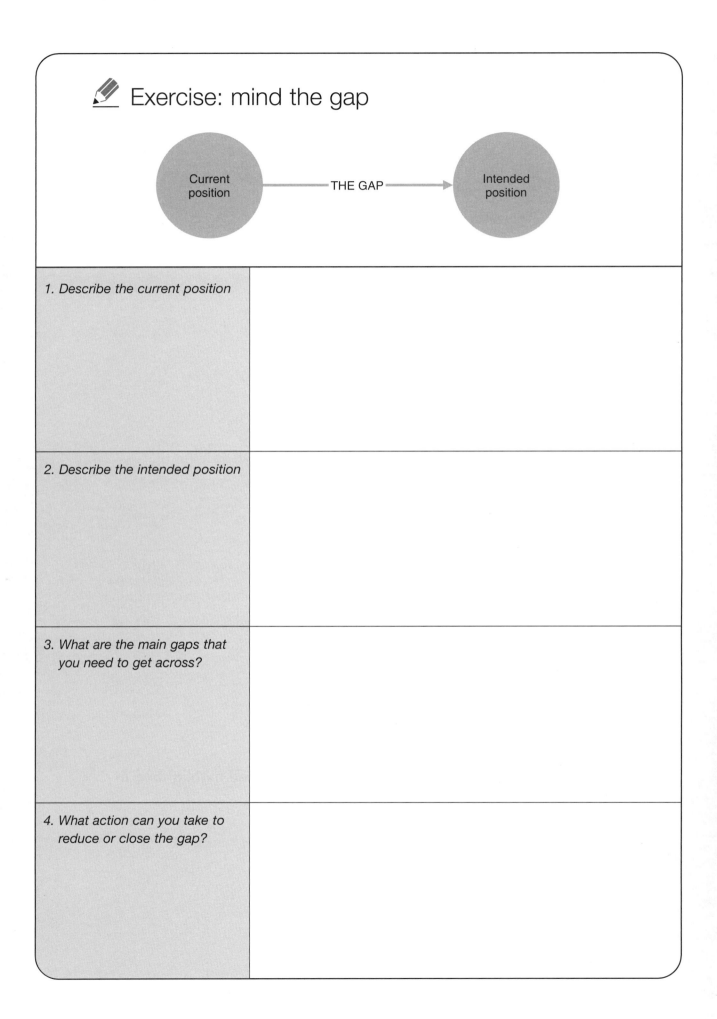

Exercise: mind the gap

Current position — THE GAP → Intended position

1. Describe the current position	
2. Describe the intended position	
3. What are the main gaps that you need to get across?	
4. What action can you take to reduce or close the gap?	

✎ Exercise: learning from the past: identifying critical success factors

This exercise is designed to encourage discussion that will identify what behaviours, actions and factors lead to success. The first step is to identify a number of recent events or episodes that are regarded as successful. Once identified, discussion can then go on to identify what were the factors that made them successful. The final stage is to see if and how these factors could be developed and replicated in other areas.

	Episode 1:	*Episode 2:*	*Episode 3:*
What was the occurrence?			
What happened and how was it successful?			

Reflecting on the issues:

What were the critical factors that contributed to this success?	
How did the people responsible for it act?	
How was it managed or planned?	
What can we learn from it?	
How can we use this experience in the future?	

Exercise: developing critical success factors

Critical success factor	Actions	Measures (key performance indicators)	Overall responsibility

Chapter ten
Putting the plan on paper

Putting the business plan on paper is an important task. The document needs to be concise, to present the plans for the organisation and to convince people that the organisation is credible. It has to be of use both externally and internally.

The business plan must give an honest appraisal of an organisation's development to date: it should note weaknesses and setbacks as well as strengths and achievements. Some of the most effective plans are those that give a full picture of an organisation and clearly indicate the action that the management will be taking to improve performance where it has been lacking.

An experienced manager of a funding body described what he looked for in a business plan:

> I look for four things. First, clarity about what the organisation is for. What's the big idea behind it? What real difference is it trying to make? Second, a well-thought-through and realistic strategy. How can the organisation use its limited resources to make the maximum impact for its beneficiaries? A strategy that simply goes for 'more of the same and keeping going' isn't good enough. Third, that the organisation has the management in place to achieve its strategy: they have thought through what is needed to do it, properly costed it and are a safe investment. And fourth, ambition with a touch of realism.

> Sometimes it is quite a task to wade through a plan to find these things.

This chapter covers:

- the structure of the business plan;
- the plan's style and format;
- the executive summary;
- putting the plan together.

The structure of a business plan

The following table outlines the sections needed in the plan, the contents of these sections and some key pointers, plus which chapters to refer to for more information.

Section	Content	Key pointers
An executive summary	A brief outline of the vision, mission, values and context: a one-page three-minute read. It should highlight the proposed direction and key benefits and make the case for the organisation.	● Make sure it is no more than one page. ● Highlight the key messages. ● See page 200.
Introduction and mission	The organisation's vision, mission and values in full with an explanation of the purpose and duration of the plan.	● It can be useful to include outputs and outcomes. ● See Chapter 5.
The organisation's background	A brief history of the organisation with basic and factual information to help readers get a picture of your organisation, including: ● the legal status of the organisation; ● any relationship to a parent organisation; ● the scale of the operation: where you work and with whom, and what you do; ● the size of the operation: including the number of projects, staff and the organisation's turnover.	● Give factual information only. ● Don't create a mini annual report: provide just basic information to give readers background context.
Internal performance	● A short review of the organisation to date, stressing strengths, achievements and external recognition. ● Evidence of having looked at the organisation and its activities objectively, for example by acknowledging weaknesses as well as strengths.	● A SWOT analysis is a useful way to display an honest appraisal of weaknesses. ● If your organisation is in a benchmarking league table, list your current ranking. ● See Chapter 6.
Future trends	● An outline of how the organisation sees its future environment developing. ● The likely needs of service users. ● Evidence that thought has been given to likely external developments.	● Demonstrate that the organisation is in touch with changes in its wider environment and has thought through potential implications. ● See Chapter 6.

Strategic direction	<ul><li>The main future direction of the organisation's work and the assumptions which underpin the chosen direction.</li><li>The main priorities.</li><li>What will be different.</li></ul>	<ul><li>Show that the organisation has a focus, a clear direction and realistic priorities.</li><li>See Chapter 7.</li></ul>
Strategic aims	<ul><li>A statement of aims for the medium term.</li><li>The plans for implementing the delivery of the plan in terms of outcomes, key measures, outputs, etc.</li></ul>	<ul><li>The specific objectives for each aim could be listed or a brief summary of them given.</li><li>See Chapter 7.</li></ul>
Resource implications	<ul><li>An explanation of how the plan will be funded.</li><li>The business model.</li><li>Income and expenditure projections for first year and estimates for following years.</li><li>A list of financial assumptions behind the plan with a statement of key financial policy (such as a pricing policy) and evidence of efficient management (such as a cash-flow forecast).</li></ul>	<ul><li>Demonstrate that the organisation is taking a strategic approach to funding.</li><li>Show that the organisation has fully costed its plans and is financially viable.</li><li>See Chapter 8.</li></ul>
Change and risk implications	<ul><li>The feasibility of new initiatives.</li><li>How the organisation needs to develop or change in order to meet the plan.</li><li>Any areas of work that will be dropped or phased out should be noted.</li><li>A list of organisational (skills, policies, etc.), legal or any other key implications.</li><li>The critical success factors that need to be in place to deliver the plan.</li><li>A risk-management summary.</li></ul>	<ul><li>See Chapter 9.</li></ul>
Track record of organisation	<ul><li>Evidence of past achievements, organisational and staff competence to make the case for the organisation by showing that it has the necessary management competence and experience to manage and deliver the plan.</li></ul>	<ul><li>List the past experience of the organisation and its key personnel.</li><li>See Chapter 9.</li></ul>
Immediate action plan	<ul><li>Timed action for the first steps in the plan.</li></ul>	<ul><li>See Chapter 11.</li></ul>

Style and format are important

Careful thought needs to be given to the style and format of the business plan. It is useful to list the main messages (no more than five) that you want the plan to convey and organise the rest of the information and evidence around them.

Some business plans suffer from being written by people who are so close to the organisation that they cannot see it as an outsider would. Obvious pieces of information are forgotten, jargon is used and assumptions made. It is worthwhile to ask someone not associated with the organisation to read it through or edit it.

The tone of the document is important. It needs to convey the message that the organisation has gone through a rigorous process to arrive at it. To help convey this, the language must be practical and active. It is not a bland policy statement. A useful exercise is to read through the draft and check that all statements can be backed up by evidence and also that targets and commitments are clearly included in the detailed plan.

The executive summary

The executive summary is particularly important because it gives a first impression which can often greatly influence the future considerations of potential backers. It is easy to get lost in the detail of the plan itself; in such instances it is important to remember that many potential backers use the summary or, in its absence, a two-minute glance through the full document, to get 'a feel of the plan'.

The executive summary should highlight the main features of the organisation, set out its strategic direction and make clear what is expected from others. If you struggle to summarise the main message of the plan or are not able to set out the key headlines, then it is likely that implementation will be hard as key people such as staff and funders will also miss the main message. The 'elevator test', outlined on page 204, can help you to distil the main messages of your plan.

Example: a one-page executive summary – Eastside Business Agency

The Eastside Business Agency is a registered charity and established as a company limited by guarantee. Founded in 1987, we operate on the east side of the city: an area of declining employment, high adult unemployment and social deprivation. Our mission is to support a viable and sustainable local economy and to provide high-quality advice, training and support to emerging or newly created small businesses. In carrying out this mission we will ensure that the highest standards of quality and equal opportunities apply throughout.

Our team of seven staff members provide:

- initial advice for those considering self-employment;
- practical help with business start-ups, training and consultancy;
- joint marketing and continued contact with new businesses in their first three years of operation.

We deal with an average of 45 new or potential new businesses at any one time. A recent evaluation shows that we have helped to create 126 new businesses in Eastside which employ nearly 300 people. Thirty-nine per cent of our clients are from the Black and Asian communities.

We have developed successful partnerships and funding arrangements with the City Council, the Eastside College and the Eastside Regeneration Partnership. One of the high points of last year was receiving the award of the Investors in People standard in recognition of our commitment to staff development.

This two-year business plan has two central themes: the consolidation of the Agency's work and the development of new services to help established businesses survive the difficult trading climate.

The plan puts forward four strategic aims. The first two will consolidate our existing advice, counselling and information services and continue our popular business training programme. Our third aim is to encourage practical cooperation and joint marketing of existing businesses. Our fourth aim is to pilot new ways of providing assistance to businesses approaching or facing insolvency. This is a new area of work for us and is in response to growing enquiries from our clients.

The plan sets out how this strategy can be achieved with backing at an equivalent level from our current partners, the gradual closure of our grants advisory service and the creation of a new post of marketing support manager.

We are now an established and proven agency working within the inner city. This plan sets out a two-year future for our continued success.

Putting the plan together

Here are some tips for putting the business plan together.

1 Always suggest a solution to a problem

Acknowledge problems and setbacks, but show that you have learnt from them and have a plan. For example:

Following a review of our high volunteer turnover rates, we have instituted a programme of volunteer support procedures to ensure that all volunteers get an effective and appropriate level of support and supervision.

2 Think about the needs of different readers

Think about how the plan will meet the needs of different readers including staff, volunteers, funders, and potential funders. Ensure that it answers the issues that concern them.

3 Use active language

The plan needs to come across as a dynamic document that will lead to real work. Avoid passive language. Say 'we will...' rather than 'it is intended that...' Use short words rather than long ones.

4 Use charts and diagrams to illustrate or emphasise points

Many readers will simply flip through the plan, so using a SWOT diagram or a chart showing the balance of intended income can help to catch the eye and draw them into the document.

5 Beware of using abbreviations or insider-speak

Check for use of abbreviations – preferably spell them out, or if you must use them qualify them at first use – and don't use organisational shorthand or jargon.

6 Use the executive summary

The executive summary should set out the main points that you want readers to remember from the plan. Write the summary after you have drafted the whole plan. If the executive summary is hard to write it might be because the plan itself is vague and unclear.

7 Highlight the first steps

If a plan sets out a big and bold direction, ensure that the first steps for taking action are clear. These first steps should help people to understand what is going to happen.

8 Attach measures

Add credibility to the plan by showing how the strategy will be measured and monitored.

9 Edit it as a whole document

Often different people draft different bits of the plan. The director drafts the strategy, the finance manager does the costings and programme staff write their work plans. This is good and can help to make the plan a team effort. However, it is useful if one person is given responsibility for editing the text to check for consistency of style and to make sure the whole document flows.

10 Ask someone outside the organisation to be a critical reader

Ask someone who is not part of the organisation to comment critically on the final draft. Ask them to say what they think the main headline messages are as well as commenting on the document's structure and style.

Case study: protecting your information

It can be problematic if a business plan that could be of value to a competitor is released. The manager of a training centre experienced this problem when required to produce a business plan for a tender to manage a government training programme:

> Our business plan contained details of how we cost our work, staffing levels and management arrangements. This information represented the product of years of work in trying to get the service right. We have always worked in a very open way, but I would be unhappy if some of the agencies we now compete with had sight of it. We did submit it, but on the condition that its circulation was restricted.

The business plan itself followed a format similar to the one set out in this chapter. It was made available to funders and purchasers, who could request any further information. A one-page executive summary was attached to the business plan as a covering document and also used in presentations about the organisation. It was particularly useful for dealing with politicians who had little time to read the full document and only really needed to know the overall direction. The summary document was a freely available publication circulated to the public. The action plan was described by one staff member as a 'management bible' and was regularly used by staff who were working to the plan.

🖉 Exercise: the elevator test

This exercise, borrowed from commercial venture capitalists, is a simple and challenging way of testing how clear you are about the main messages of your business plan.

Imagine that you are visiting a potential funder at their office to talk over your new business plan. At the reception you press the button to summon the lift. As you wait for the lift you are joined by the chief executive of the funding body. The chief executive has met you before and asks why you are visiting their organisation. You explain that you are dropping off a copy of your new business plan in the hope that it might lead to funding.

The lift arrives and you both enter it. The chief executive comments that she will not probably have time to read your plan and asks you what the main messages of your business plan are and why they should back it.

The lift journey will take three to four minutes. You are unlikely to get another chance to talk directly to the chief executive. What would you say?

Review

How easy was it to identify the main messages?

What are the main messages that you want readers of the plan to remember?

How well does the plan present them and highlight them?

✎ Evaluating your plan

Make notes about your own plan in the spaces provided.

How does the plan create a sense of purpose or mission for which all people involved in the organisation can work? Is this sense of purpose presented clearly?

Are all the strategic aims and detailed objectives in the plan consistent with the mission?

Do you have a good understanding of the potential changes and trends in your external environment? How could these changes affect your organisation's future?

On a continuum ranging from 'bleakly pessimistic' to 'wildly optimistic', evaluate the main decisions and aims within the plan.

Bleakly pessimistic   Wildly optimistic

▶ • ◀

Do any of these decisions and aims cause you concern? If so, why?

On a continuum ranging from 'wild guess' to 'guaranteed forecast' evaluate the main forecasts and projections in the plan.

Wild guess   Guaranteed forecast

Do any of these forecasts and projections cause you concern? If so, why?

On a continuum of 'mission impossible' to 'will be easy to achieve' evaluate the specific objectives and work commitments set out in the plan.

Mission impossible   Will be easy to achieve

Do any of these specific objectives and work commitments cause you concern? If so, why?

How does the plan address any concerns or risks?

List the five main messages that you would like readers of the plan to retain:

1

2

3

4

5

How clearly does the plan convey these points?

How will you know if the plan has worked? What feedback and monitoring systems will you use?

What will the first steps be after agreeing the plan? What is the immediate action plan?

Chapter eleven
Making it happen

We have a strategic plan. It's called doing things.

Herb Kelleher, former CEO of Southwest Airlines

It is sadly common for organisations to invest time in the planning process, produce a business plan and then just file it away. It is forgotten, gathering dust on a shelf until it has to be worked on again.

This can happen for a number of reasons:

- The plan never dealt with the realities of the organisation. It is all about how people would like it to be in a perfect world.

- The process of putting the plan together never engaged the people who needed to implement it. The managers and/or external consultants who drove the planning process didn't create a feeling of ownership throughout the organisation.

- The plan itself is fine, but managers have neither the time nor the skills to manage the changes involved.

This chapter addresses the following issues to help you to ensure that the plan doesn't get left on the shelf.

1. Planning the implementation of the business plan: how to turn strategic aims into delivery plans.

2. Managing organisational change.

3. Managing performance: ensuring that things get done, including how trustees and managers can ensure that the plan happens.

4. How to monitor the plan's progress.

5. When and how to update the plan.

Planning the implementation of the business plan

The following case study demonstrates how to turn strategic aims into delivery plans.

Case study: after the plan... more planning

The managers of Hillgate Care, a well-established charity which provides care and support schemes for a range of adults with learning disabilities, recognised that their newly agreed business plan would require radical changes. The new plan was based on the recognition that the organisation needed to change, embrace best practice and also follow up opportunities to expand into neighbouring local authorities. The plan had the following main strategic priorities:

- To encourage and support the involvement and participation of the service users throughout.
- To broaden the income base by expanding into neighbouring local authorities.
- To develop a community business to create employment for some service users.
- To develop a home support service to assist some service users to live independently.

The management team agreed to set up three implementation groups to draw up action plans and lead the work. The three groups were:

1. **A business/service development group:** this group was charged with developing a business case (see page 118) for each new service and for setting up a marketing campaign to develop new business.
2. **A staff development group:** the team recognised that the plan would require new skills in the organisation. This group was given the responsibility of setting up a staff training programme focused on service user involvement and also a programme for staff moving from a central to an outreach role.
3. **An organisation group:** the organisation group was given the responsibility of ensuring that the organisation's infrastructure could cope with growth. The group developed an action plan to look at what new systems and processes would be needed to support expansion.

All the groups were established as fixed-term projects for three months. Members of staff were appointed to each group and were asked to give a minimum of three days and a maximum of six days to work on the group. Each group was asked to prepare an action plan for its work which was approved by the management committee. The action plans were structured around six key issues.

- **Success criteria:** How will we judge success? What is the overall goal?
- **Key activities:** An outline of the programme of work needed.
- **Work breakdown schedule:** A timed programme of the key tasks, events and activities (as outlined in the following section).
- **Resource needs:** A statement of financial, human and other resources needed to accomplish the plan.
- **Milestones:** A plan setting out key review dates.
- **Responsibility:** Named lead responsibility for implementing the plan.

The charity's director commented on what she had learnt as a result of the process:

What I realised was the importance of moving from strategy to detail. In the past we've become stuck at the level of mission and overall strategy. This time we realised that to get things moving we had to get serious about planning the implementation of the plan.

Another main learning point was how important it is to involve staff in planning implementation. By involving staff from across the organisation in drawing up the implementation plans people felt encouraged and communicated with and, most importantly, they felt that they owned the plan.

We also realised from past experience that things just do not happen unless responsibility is allocated, so we went through every line of the plan and made sure that an individual was responsible for ensuring that action was taken on every commitment and target. We've found that attaching a name to a plan and ensuring that progress is checked makes sure that things get done.

Work breakdown schedules

A simple technique for planning the details of the implementation is to use the strategic aims to identify the different tasks involved in the strategy and turn them into an action plan. For example, a health promotion project might decide that one of its strategic aims is 'to encourage and support schoolteachers in promoting healthy eating habits'.

The first step is to list all the tasks necessary to implement this priority. A useful way of doing this – sometimes called a 'work breakdown schedule' – is to draw up a list of all the tasks. At this stage, the size of the task or the order in which it should be tackled is not important. Figure 11.1 provides an example of a work breakdown schedule.

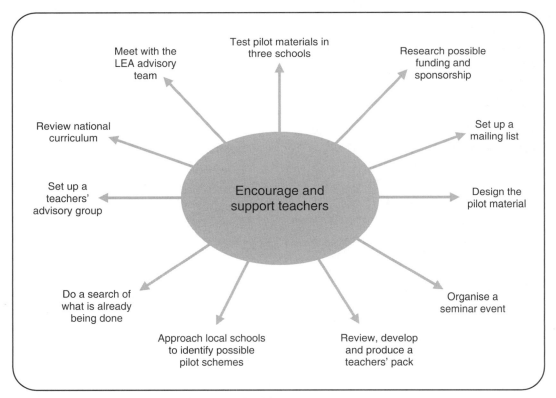

Fig. 11.1   Tasks for a work breakdown schedule

Once all the tasks have been identified the next step is to put them into a logical order by working out which tasks are dependent on others happening first, i.e. to put together the schedule itself.

Task order	Task	Start date	Time needed	Resources or action needed	Responsible	Notes
1	Do a search of what is already being done	Week 1	1 day	Internet	Sally	Produce brief for team
2	Review the national curriculum	Week 1	1 day	Internet	Bob	Produce briefing paper
3	Meet with the LEA advisory team	Week 2	Half a day	Time	Bob and Sally	Do after 1 and 2
4	Approach local schools to identify possible pilot projects	Week 2	2 days	Send a mailing via the LEA; phone calls	Bob, Sally and Helen	Do after 3; get LEA to supply contacts
5	Research possible funding and sponsorship	Week 1	1 day	Funding directories or websites	Helen	Make file note
6	Set up a teachers' advisory group	Week 3	3 days	Team to suggest possible people	Sally	Plan for first meeting in week 6
7	Design the pilot material	Week 4	8 days	Computer; books; budget of £250	Bob	Do after 1

8	Try out the pilot materials in three schools	Week 8	6 days	Materials; feedback sheets	Bob to deliver the material; Sally to evaluate the level of the materials' success	Report to advisory group in week 10
9	Review, develop and produce a teachers' pack	Week 10	20 days	Computer; designer; printing; budget of £500	Bob and Sally with input from pilot teachers	Drafts ready in week 12; back from printers in week 14
10	Set up a mailing list	Week 15	2 days	Contact lists from the team mailing database; pack materials	Helen	Mail out pack and invitations to launch in week 15
11	Organise seminar event	Week 16	4 days	Book venue Do programme mail out; budget of £700	Bob and Helen	Seminar in week 18

Case study: the plan on a page

The planning group at the Downside Community Health Initiative realised that most of their staff and volunteer team would only skim-read the 14-page business plan that had just been agreed. To overcome this and to ensure that the strategy was understood they produced a one-page plan.

The document sets out the vision, mission and values, highlights the five strategic aims and then describes the operational plan for year one. The operational plan is divided into ongoing work and projects. Every year the team will update the operational plan to keep it relevant.

The one-page plan is displayed throughout the organisation and is regularly used in supervision and team meetings to check that all activities fit with the plan.

The plan on a page: The Downside Community Health Initiative

Overall vision and mission	Five strategic aims:	Operational plans for year 1–current:	Operational plans for year 1–current projects
Vision Healthy and happy people in the Downside community. **Mission** To motivate, support and enable local people to make positive lifestyle choices which will improve their health and increase their potential to enjoy life to the full. **Values** ● To deliver high-quality services ● To work in partnership ● To be accountable ● To be fair, open and honest ● To be accessible to all ● To listen and learn	1. To work with partners to increase the relevance and accessibility of local health services in meeting community needs.	● Run the Downside Forum. ● Produce the *Downside Health Guide* pamphlet and website. ● Convene voluntary sector health forums. ● Train and support 80 health advocates.	● Research into local health gaps. ● Carry out six access audits.
	2. To develop accessible schemes and projects that encourage an active and healthy lifestyle.	● Manage the gym on prescription service for 350 local people. ● Support the Downside over-55s walking group. ● Manage and support 22 urban gardens.	● Investigate the feasibility of setting up a food co-op. ● Run the annual Downside 'good health weekend'.
	3. To implement programmes that increase awareness, and reduce the effects, of smoking and alcohol abuse.	● Set up 18 Quit Smoking support groups. ● Run two Drink Wise campaigns. ● Develop and run pilot schemes of a schools programme on alcohol in six secondary schools.	● Action a research project with partners on street drinking. ● Set up a pilot project using social media tools.
	4. To reduce the effects of unemployment and poverty on mental and community health.	● Run group work and one-to-one sessions as required. ● Deliver 12 stress-buster programmes ● Continue with the It's Good to Talk programme.	● Develop referral routes with GPs. ● Design and deliver a training event for other agencies.
	5. To be a strong, sustainable and independent organisation.	● Maintain and develop effective partnerships with key commissioners and partners. ● Demonstrate best organisational practice throughout. ● Join forces with the Clinical Commissioning group.	● Commission a full evaluation of our work. ● Explore ways of generating income through trading.

Gantt charts

A useful way of displaying the plan in an easily viewable way is as a Gantt chart. A Gantt chart is a simple way of showing what should be happening at a particular time; it highlights potential problems and bottlenecks where there will be too much happening at one time. It also allows you to visibly monitor progress and achievements. Figure 11.2 provides an example of a Gantt chart in use. The numbers represent weeks.

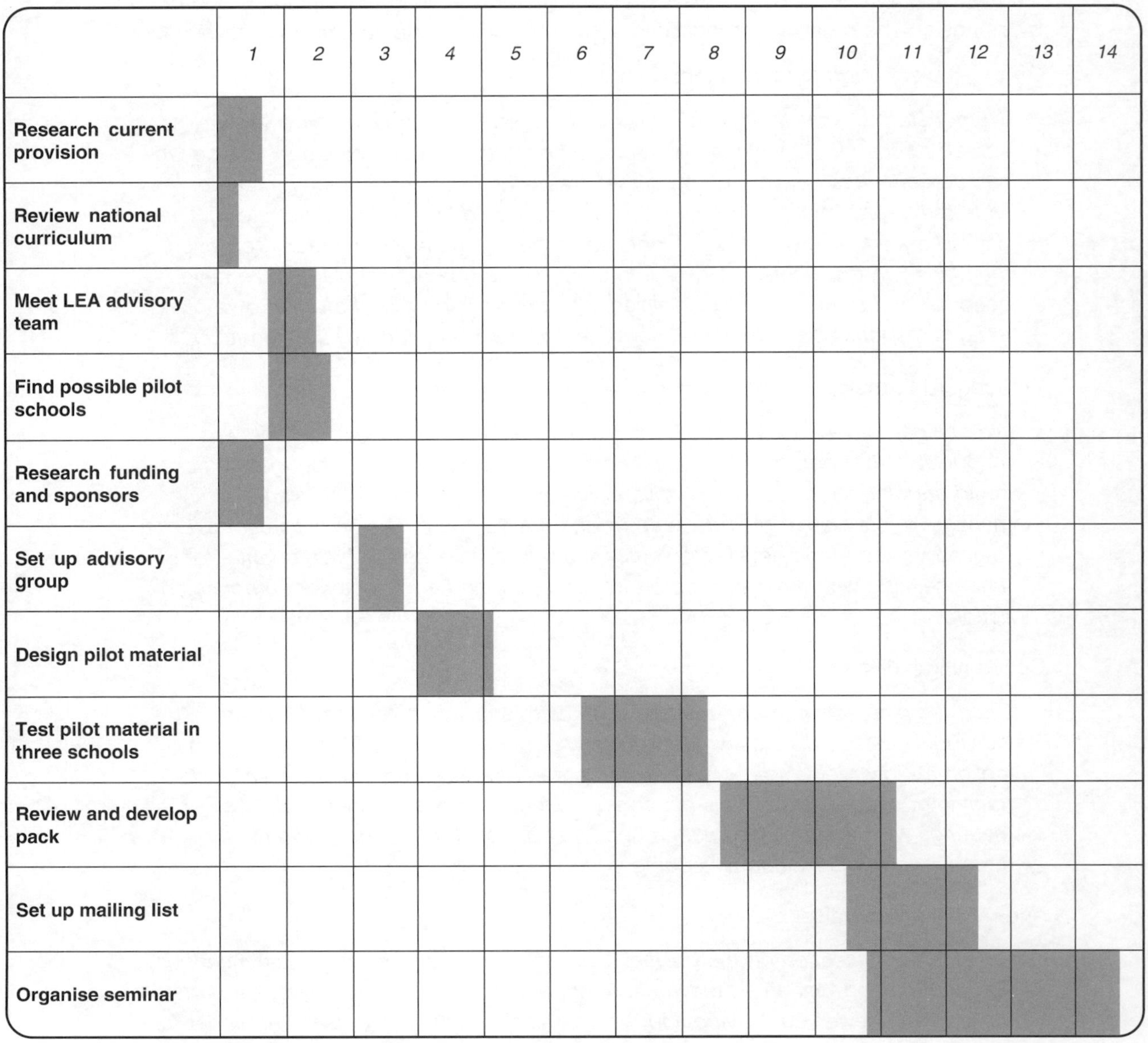

	1	2	3	4	5	6	7	8	9	10	11	12	13	14
Research current provision	■													
Review national curriculum	■													
Meet LEA advisory team		■												
Find possible pilot schools		■												
Research funding and sponsors	■													
Set up advisory group			■											
Design pilot material				■										
Test pilot material in three schools						■	■							
Review and develop pack									■	■				
Set up mailing list											■	■		
Organise seminar												■	■	■

Fig. 11.2 Simple example of a Gantt chart

Case study: implementing the business plan

The members of an environmental organisation's management team spent time changing how they organised the delivery of their new strategic plan. In the past, its implementation was not planned. As one manager commented, 'once the final draft of the plan was agreed by our board it was as if people assumed that things would happen by osmosis'. The organisation adopted some new approaches to improve the situation.

On the subject of drafting the plan:

We got staff to write their bit of the plan. For example, at a strategic level we agreed to change how we involved and supported our member groups. Once we had agreed what we were doing in the strategy we asked our field workers to write the operational plan to set out how they would implement the strategy. They drafted a work plan with clear targets and then the management team approved the plans. On the whole, it worked. In the past the operational plan would have been handed to them, but we realised that getting people to draft their own plan assigns responsibility – they are more likely to work on it if they have produced it.

With regard to management decisions:

We delegated decision-making. We told our resources manager that she was responsible for upgrading our technology, she had control of the budget and she could appoint and supervise suppliers. She saw it as her bit of the plan. Her line manager's role was to provide support and advise and check on progress, but not to get involved in the detail. Previously she would have had to have spent a lot of time checking with managers before she could spend any money or authorise any action.

Concerning individual support:

Once the plan was agreed, managers met with each member of staff on an individual basis to discuss what the plan would mean for them. These meetings looked at how their role might change, agreed priorities and also identified what training or support individuals might need. One of the main benefits of these meetings was that it helped us to check that people really understood the direction the organisation was going in.

And regarding appraisals:

We included a section on the business plan in our six-monthly appraisal meetings. The contribution that an employee had made to implementing the relevant parts of the plan was reviewed. Having it in the appraisal system was a useful reminder for both managers and staff.

Managing organisational change

Inevitably, a new strategy and plan will involve some kind of change. Change can be a creative and exciting process, but it often causes anxiety, disruption and even conflict.

First-order and second-order change

An interesting idea to consider here is the difference between first-order change and second-order change. First-order change is when an organisation accommodates a change within its current culture and manner of working and operating. It adapts and incorporates. Second-order change is when an organisation radically changes its way of operating, its culture and style, and is therefore more disruptive to the organisation.

First-order change is needed in general – it is what happens when you find ways to do things more efficiently, and it results in incremental improvements that fit within the organisation's existing ways of working and culture. In this way, it is not a particularly disruptive form of change.

Finding new ways of working, developing new models and adapting to a fast-changing environment fall into the category of second-order change and this means changes in how you organise, think and manage. This is the kind of change that a new strategic direction can entail.

The following advice is suggested to help managers to deal with a second-order change process:

Start early

As outlined in Chapter 4, if people are involved in planning the strategy and accept that the process was a genuinely collaborative one, there is more of a chance that they will work with or at least understand and accept the new strategic direction. Ensure that the process is open and that change is not just foisted on people.

Explain the context

It is important that people see what is behind the change and what is driving it. It is worthwhile spending time with people explaining the external landscape and how it presents opportunities and threats for the organisation. It is dangerous to assume that people understand or are even aware of the external context in which the organisation works and how it is changing.

Acknowledge uncertainty

Most change in organisations is not a simple linear line of 'here's where we are', 'here's where we are going to be' and 'here's the exact journey we are going to take'. Often it's a case of leaving A, but not being quite sure where exactly B is. You need to be clear and honest with people about the uncertainty and risks involved in a change process.

Make it personal

In implementing a strategy it is useful to think what it might mean for individual staff members. How might their roles change? What skills will they need to develop? What will be different in how they do their job?

The management team of a youth agency agreed that managers would meet with each staff member to talk through the potential implications of its new strategy. One area manager commented on his experience of doing this:

> *Having to explain to our 18-hours-a-week centre caretaker what the agency's new commitment to 'service user choice, engagement and empowerment' meant for him, in particular how to make it relevant to his job, was really challenging at first. However, it was a useful process that showed that he was a key member of the team who often had more direct contact with service users than anyone else.*

Manage the pace of the process

Change takes time, but it also needs a sense of momentum. Be careful of moving at the pace of the slowest and subjecting the change to long, drawn-out discussion and consultation: the plan can easily lose direction and be stalled. Manage and direct any consultation carefully. Which things are up for consultation and which are not? (See chapter 4 for more information on consulting people effectively.)

Check that the process doesn't regress

Managing a change process well takes sustained effort and determination. People and organisations can have a tendency to revert to how things were as soon as things get tough.

A housing agency was committed to an organisational change process that involved staff working in integrated teams, communicating better and being quicker and more flexible at solving tenants' problems rather than hiding behind procedures. A director described what happened:

> *For the first few months our strategy really worked well and started to make a difference. Then we started to hit some snags: our IT systems weren't up to it; small problems, such as whose budget something comes out of, were escalated into major problems. You could see people retreating into the old ways of thinking 'that's not my job...' and 'it's the fault of the xyz team'. As managers, we took our eye off the ball and failed to demonstrate our personal commitment to seeing it through.*

To avoid this trap it is important for managers to show their commitment to stick with the plan, especially when things get tough.

From strategy to culture

The following examples show how three organisations tackled the changes in organisational culture brought about by a new strategic direction and how they undertook change programmes in order to create new cultures that supported the strategy.

1. Bridgate Care Charity: open for business

Background

The Bridgate Care Charity had traditionally relied upon a mix of grants and fundraising to cover the costs of providing support to people with care needs living at home. Staff had very little involvement in the funding process. Service users had little say in what was provided. At worst a 'take it or leave it' attitude existed.

Strategic direction

The trustees felt that their traditional charity model was under threat. Traditional grant funders were moving towards commissioning. The charity was more likely to be issued with a unit contract for a specific piece of work. An increasing number of service users desiring choice meant that some service users would be given direct control over what service they purchased. Some service users might be able to pay for additional services.

New or intended culture

The charity needed to become more systematic and enterprising but at the same time retain its principles and values. Services had to become more flexible and adaptive to the varied needs and wants of service users.

The *individuals* who use and, in some cases, pay for services needed to be given respect and real choice, and team leaders needed to be able to respond to requests and organise and change care packages quickly.

Change programme elements

A series of workshops were delivered by managers to explain why a new way of working was needed.

The job role of team leader was revised to give the team leader greater managerial control and decision-making power. This was backed up with personal development programmes to help people make the change.

Staff worked in six service review teams to look at how services could be made more flexible and personal and marketed better. The charity's head office introduced a business support system to help team leaders to cost and negotiate services.

2. Millway: command and control

Background

Millway is a large national charity with a headquarters (HQ) in London and nearly 40 projects throughout the UK. Traditionally the HQ has seen its role as being to direct, manage and control Millway's local projects.

Strategic direction

Millway's recently appointed Chief Executive felt that she was continually having to control infighting between the HQ and local projects. HQ staff felt that many projects were out of control and were poor at keeping to Millway's corporate systems and procedures. Local project managers were annoyed that HQ kept producing time-consuming controls and systems that made the work harder and, at best, were irrelevant. Many HQ staff had never met a service user.

New or intended culture

Millway's CEO was determined to change the management and organisational culture. She wanted to reduce the level of internal conflict and office politics. She was determined to reduce the size of the HQ (too much money that could be going into services was being spent on running the organisation).

She also wanted staff at HQ to see their role as supporting the people who deliver the organisation's services rather than controlling and overseeing them.

Change programme elements

Millway agreed a three-stage six-month campaign:

1. **Breaking down barriers:** all HQ staff were encouraged to spend a few days working at a local project. A local project leader was seconded to HQ to cover a vacancy. A special staff conference was held with the intention of reminding staff about the overall vision and mission and how their work supported it.

2. **Cutting red tape:** a task group was set up to review and challenge all procedures and systems. In two meetings it cut the number of forms that project leaders were required to submit from eighteen to six.

3. **Going local:** Millway's management team identified a series of issues and decisions that project leaders could now decide without having to ask for HQ approval. This was backed up with a training programme to enable project managers to take greater responsibility.

3. Focuscare: service users matter

Background

Focuscare provides a range of services including supported housing, care packages and personal support to people with learning disabilities.

In informal conversations with Focuscare's management team, two commissioners had commented that they felt that the organisation was weak at encouraging service users to make decisions and exercise choice about their care. They felt that a 'we know best' approach was ingrained in parts of the organisation.

Strategic direction

Informed by the feedback from commissioners, Focuscare's board and management made 'increasing the level of choice and decision-making that our service users have in the things that matter to them' a key strategic organisational priority.

New or intended culture

Focuscare wanted to create a culture in which service users were encouraged and supported to have a say or make decisions at any point of their contact with the organisation. It wanted to create a culture where being listened to, being involved and having a say would be the norm for a service user.

Focuscare also sought to develop its services and introduce a range of initiatives: from encouraging greater service-user feedback to direct service-user control.

Change programme elements

Focuscare developed a series of initiatives to demonstrate to service users and staff the personal commitment of the organisation's leadership to this. It also developed a series of competencies that set out the behaviours that service users should expect to see. This involved some staff having to unlearn traditional ways of working.

A regular service-user survey (every six months) was put in place to measure progress, and a service-users' forum was be appointed and given a budget to spend as it saw fit.

Managing performance: ensuring that things get done

A board member of a national organisation described performance management in her organisation as follows:

> *Ready, Aim, Fire! does not really apply to our organisation. We spend a lot of time getting ready: producing policies, doing training, carrying out research, talking about the process. We are forever altering our aim – agreeing strategies and writing plans – but we never get round to firing! A lot of brilliant and exciting plans simply never happen.*

In many ways writing the plan is the easy job. Getting people to take responsibility for the plan and ensuring that action is taken is the real hard work. Performance is about getting things done and often involves a change of gear from talking to getting on and doing it. To build a working culture that supports and encourages good performance, it is important to:

- have an emphasis on outcomes;
- build an atmosphere which encourages action;
- ensure that people know what is expected of them and responsibility for implementation is clearly agreed;
- promote a sense of personal responsibility;
- delegate effectively;
- allow people to get on with it;
- monitor progress;
- ensure that the strategy is still relevant;
- communicate with internal and external stakeholders.

An emphasis on outcomes

In a performance culture the emphasis is on achieving an outcome and less on the detailed methods used to get there. Work should be defined as an intended outcome rather than an activity.

Outcome	Possible activity
A self-managing and representative service-user forum.	Train and support service-user forum members.
Increased numbers of people from low-income households attending our events.	Do outreach work in disadvantaged areas.
A reduced number of household accidents suffered by elderly people.	Run an accident-prevention publicity campaign.

Outcomes are about achieving a pre-set result. The focus is on the ends and not the means. A wide range of activities and interventions could achieve the outcome of a reduced number of household accidents. Describing the outcome allows some flexibility in how to get to it. The people responsible for delivering various parts of the plan can then use tools such as work breakdown schedules and Gantt charts to plan the practical details.

A bias for action

Several management writers use the term 'a bias for action', which means building an atmosphere which is about wanting to get things done and being focused on the task. This can be about overcoming procrastination or agreeing to stop discussions and move to action. People can become trapped waiting for a perfect plan to be agreed or for everything to be in place. However, given that there is no such thing as a perfect plan, getting started with a decent plan is better than no action at all.

A crucial element of creating a bias for action is helping people feel that they have responsibility for implementing an element of the plan. The objective is to make people feel that they 'own' the elements of the plan that they will deliver. This is about creating personal responsibility, ensuring that people are recognised as being responsible and delegating responsibilities for drawing up the detail of the plan as well as delegating responsibilities for making decisions and managing budgets.

A first step is to ensure that, once the plan has been agreed, responsibility for delivery is then clearly assigned. Everyone should know what is expected of them and everyone should know what everyone else is expected to do as a result of the plan. A useful way of doing this is to go through the plan and identify every task, commitment or intention and then to allocate each one to an individual so that it is clear exactly who has the responsibility for ensuring delivery of these items. Things do not happen unless they are clearly allocated to individuals for implementation.

Case study: encouraging responsibility for implementation

The manager of a housing project described how work on the strategic plan led to a shift in the management style of his organisation:

In the past some individuals developed the art of saying a lot in strategy meetings and then going strangely quiet when we got to the bit about who was going to do things. Often all the implementation ended up on my desk. It used to feel as though it was 'my plan'.

This year was different. Once the plan was agreed I went through the document with a highlighter and identified every task, action point or thing we said we would do. I then sat down with each of the three senior workers and agreed with them which ones they would have lead responsibility for. It's now my job to check on progress and provide any support and backup. We used a Gantt chart format to display the implementation plan on our main office wall. Having clear deadlines with people's names on it all makes it feel real. We regularly update the plan to record progress and discuss at our monthly team meeting any snags that might block progress.

It is interesting how being open and determined about this has changed things. Staff now talk of it as 'our plan'. The three senior staff are now involved in implementing a strategy that cuts across the whole organisation. This has led them to see the whole picture, not just their bit, and be more corporate in how they work. My job has changed. My role is more about facilitating and supporting the implementation of the strategy, rather than doing it all.

Building performance: how trustees and managers can ensure that the plan happens

Performance management can be described as a four-stage framework, as illustrated in figure 11.3.

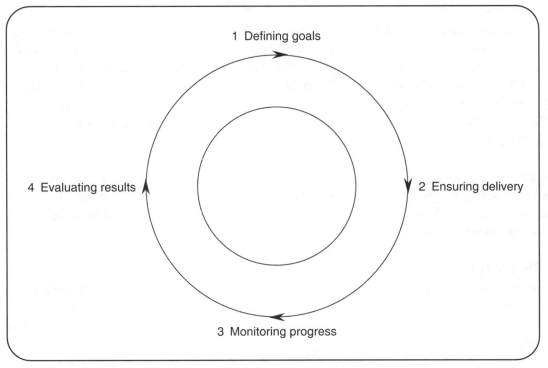

Fig. 11.3 A four-stage performance management framework

Stage one

The first stage, defining goals for individuals, is about ensuring that people understand what is being delegated to them and what is expected of them. Some things are easier to define than others. For instance, it is usually easy to define time and money: 'it needs to be ready by the end of the month; don't spend more than £400 on it'. Other factors such as quality ('it must meet service-user needs') and process issues ('service users must feel they are involved') are harder to define. Delegation must be clear and describe the required result. The person carrying out the task must know:

● what exactly they are expected to deliver;

● which resources are available to them;

● which decisions they can make.

Delegation is not just about handing out work; it is also about delegating decisions.

Stage two

At the second stage, it is important that individuals are able to get on with the task. A plan needs to be agreed and resources controlled. However, some flexibility must be allowed. Too much planning can lead to a lack of responsiveness where the plan is implemented regardless of feedback and changing circumstances, which can lead to achieving an outcome which is no longer needed. Managers will need to help people involved in delivery by coaching and providing guidance and support, but not by taking the work over.

Stage three

The third stage is about having a monitoring process that identifies progress, ensures that things are on track and flags up potential problems. Two issues are important here: first, having an early-warning system to indicate problems before they become a crisis and, second, a system that recognises progress and achievements. Forms of monitoring include:

- **Agreeing intended milestones in advance.** Milestones are key points on the road to achieving your goal. It is useful to break a bigger plan into a series of milestones and estimate when it is expected that the milestone will be met. For example, one of the early milestones in running a fundraising campaign might be to 'have recruited and trained a volunteer campaign team'.
- **Regular supervision systems.** Having regular one-to-one meetings between the person delivering the work and the supervisor is an effective way of reviewing progress and planning the next stage.
- **Formal systems.** It is useful to employ established, formal ways of planning and monitoring progress, such as using Gantt charts (see page 215). As the work is done, tasks can be marked off on the chart. This is a quick and visual way of showing that the delivery of the plan is on track.

Stage four

In the final stage, results need to be evaluated. The fact that part of the plan has been completed should be communicated both internally and externally. It also provides an opportunity to give feedback, acknowledge effort and to learn from what did and did not work.

Effective managers

The following quick tips are useful rules for managers to manage performance effectively:

Be prepared to act

It is important that managers act. Problems or failures in delivering results are often ignored in the hope that things will somehow get better. If managers do not take action, goals can drift and small problems can become crises.

Manage failure and setbacks

It is inevitable that things will go wrong – deadlines will be missed, budgets will overrun and mistakes be made. How failures are dealt with from the management down is an interesting test of an organisation's culture. Failures are frequently hidden or all the focus is on apportioning blame. In a performance culture, the emphasis needs to be on spotting and resolving the issue quickly and learning from it.

Take the right approach

In all things the style and role of managers is critical. In a performance culture a manager's role is to provide the direction and to coach and support people. It is not their role to do everything or to micro-manage every detail of the implementation of the plan.

Management committees

Trustees can play a key part in keeping the business plan alive. Committee members can bring a level of objectivity and detachment to a project, as they are not (or should not be) directly involved in day-to-day operations.

Case study: making sure it happens

An experienced chair of a trustee board describes her role in making sure that the plan is followed through.

In two organisations I have worked in there has been a sense of relief when the plan is agreed and signed off. It disappears. It is almost as if people think 'ah, now we can get back to normal'. I have adopted three tactics to combat this attitude. Firstly, the performance of the plan is a major topic at the chief officer's annual appraisal. We go through the plan and look at what they have done to ensure progress. Knowing that this is going to happen does give it some status.

Secondly, I make a point of seeing the plan as a work in progress. I regularly refer to it in trustee meetings. If an idea for a new project comes up I will ask how it fits into our strategy. As trustees we regularly go back to it.

And third, I pick out two or three commitments in the plan and make a point of asking about them. Two years ago we made a commitment in our plan to move towards more accessible opening hours. Three months in, it did not look as if this would happen, as it would involve some difficult negotiations with staff. I decided that I would push this issue. I regularly remind our managers of it and ask for progress reports. I try not to get involved in the detail of managing how to do it – that's their job.

Despite the difficulties, some improvements have been made. I honestly think that if I had not decided to champion the issue and push for changes then the plan would have fallen away.

The following ideas are all practical ways that a committee can help to encourage things to get done.

1. Regularly revisit the plan

Make sure that the business plan is discussed at committee meetings. It can be a useful tool for taking stock on progress, ensuring accountability and identifying the need for new strategies.

2. Make sure managers keep to the plan

The committee can help managers to deliver the plan by ensuring that they use it in their work and report back to the committee with progress reports. The plan should provide a guide for future development and action.

3. Monitor key performance indicators for the plan

The process of measurement often helps to ensure implementation. Either trustees and/or management can set key performance indicators. Trustee involvement and the regular collection, circulation and analysis of performance information will help to identify progress and also act as an early-warning system for potential problems and barriers.

4. Set aside review sessions for the plan

The committee should review the plan at least once a year to check that the strategy is still relevant and being acted on.

5. Highlight successes

When elements of the plan have been successfully completed make a point of letting people know. The process of recording progress and sharing success can enhance morale internally and also increase the confidence of external stakeholders such as funders.

6. Circulate the plan to new committee members

As new people join the committee, ensure that they are given the plan and have an opportunity to talk it through. It can be a valuable way of learning about the organisation and understanding what the organisation is trying to do, and can avoid going over old ground when trying to move ahead with the new plan..

7. Focus on the plan's key priorities: don't allow your strategic direction to drift

Keep the plan's main priorities firmly on your agenda. It is easy for an organisation to drift from issue to issue or be driven by other people's priorities. Watch out for good ideas which will tempt you off-track, urgent opportunities and any other factors which will reduce your focus, and say 'no' to them. Make sure that everyone in the organisation understands the strategy and carefully manage the temptation to add things in. If you need to change the strategy do so formally, making clear what is coming out of it as well as what is going in.

The following case study shows how the leader of an organisation can help people to focus on the plan's key priorities and keep the plan on track.

Case study: stick with it

A long-standing director of a health charity commented on how easy it is go off on tangents:

> Sometimes it feels as if my organisation suffers from a kind of strategic attention deficit disorder. It doesn't take much to knock us off our plan. Our head of fundraising is forever coming up with new proposals and identifying new places to bid to. Quite a lot of our staff are very attracted to new ideas and want to do 'the next big thing'. In the past few years we have allowed ourselves to be pulled in lots of different directions often as a result of chasing funding. And when things get tough, people lose interest and prefer to work on new ideas.

> I see part of my role as ensuring that we keep focused and to remind people what we have said we are going to do in our strategy. Now and again I have to pull people in and say no to new ideas. I recognise that there is a balancing act between responding to new opportunities and ideas and following through what you have said you were going to do. I think in the past we have been guilty of taking on far too much, jumping from one thing to another and not really following things through. We came close to having a reputation for being superficial and opportunistic. I am trying to shape a culture where we will still be responsive, but will stick with our agreed strategic direction and commitments.

Monitoring the progress of a plan

A simple way to monitor the implementation of the plan is to use a traffic light system. Progress on every aim, commitment and target is labelled against a traffic light:

 ## Red

- No or very little progress has been made
- No results

 ## Amber

- Progress in hand
- Not complete yet

Green

- Successfully completed
- A result!

Case study: monitoring progress

A campaigning organisation used the traffic light system to monitor the implementation of their plan. Here's an excerpt from their report:

	Status	Comments	Action
Set up Scottish office	Red	• Staff shortages. • Cost of offices greater than predicted.	• Director to revise budget. • Report on progress and options to the board in June.
Develop network of contacts in each parliamentary constituency	Amber	• Contacts in 218 constituencies so far. • Taking longer than we expected.	• Concentrate on key marginals. • Produce lobbying material for contacts to use.
Establish alliance of similar organisations	Amber	• First meeting held. • Launch event planned for the summer.	• Put article in newsletter. • Review at September board meeting.
Revamp, redesign and relaunch campaign bulletin	Amber	• Redesign completed. • Awaiting feedback on the design.	• Complete consultation in three weeks.
Identify supporters in parliament	Green	• Cross-parliamentary group being formed. • Successful Westminster reception held.	• Put article in newsletter. • Director to report on what actions need to be taken next.

Once you have judged the level of progress on each activity, action plans can be drawn up. For the Red items, some analysis might be needed. Why has no progress been made? Is the aim no longer relevant? Have circumstances changed that now make the plan impossible, more difficult or even undesirable? If you are to press on with the Red items, what do you need to do differently? Do you need a different implementation plan? Closer supervision, more active support and tighter monitoring might be needed. If you decide to cancel a Red item and not to go ahead with it, then you need to revise the plan and reallocate the resources and time originally budgeted for.

When you look at the Amber items you need to check whether they are where you expected them to be. Is there a danger of things slipping or overrunning? It is worthwhile checking that the next actions are clearly agreed and allocated.

The Green items should be acknowledged, recorded and celebrated. Progress can create more progress. It is useful to actively communicate that progress has been made and that the plan is taking shape.

When to update the plan

There can be a tendency to see business plans as being carved in stone: once agreed, they cannot be altered over the course of their lives. In reality all plans need to be updated and, if necessary, changed. Business plans may need revising for the following reasons:

- Unplanned and unforeseen external developments happen in the life of the plan. For instance, a major international disaster might require an immediate response from a relief agency. The disaster might also change future funding projections and intended work plans.

- The assumptions upon which the plan was built are no longer valid or the thinking behind the plan no longer holds water. For example, a surprise election result might change the political direction and priorities of a local authority and so past assumptions about levels of support might need to be rethought.

- An important opportunity may present itself which does not emerge in line with the planning timetable. For example, your organisation might be approached to work in partnership on a particular project which would significantly increase service-user access. However, remember that an attractive opportunity can take your organisation off course, so ensure that any new opportunity fits with your strategic direction and warrants a change of plan.

- The resources available to an organisation change. Fundraising projections may not work out or assumed resources become unavailable. For instance, a charity with a large investment fund might find its income projections are altered by changes in stock market performance.

- There is a poor or negative response to the plan. Reactions to the plan from key groups such as staff, service users or funders might be so negative or unsupportive as to merit a rethink of the organisation's strategy and priorities.

- There is new work that needs to be done. A regional manager of a national charity described how, despite having a well-established planning system and an agreed plan, local managers were expected to fit in new work and find the time to respond to new demands. This led to overwork, teams and individuals being overstretched and a feeling that the formal planning process lacked credibility, as agreed plans were either ignored or overwritten. To prevent this sort of crisis management, take stock, review the plan and deliberately agree what needs to change.

Management committee meetings

Management committee meetings can be a good place to identify instances when the plan may need to be updated.

Build strategy into all meetings

It is easy for a committee to spend all of its time on day-to-day reporting and operational matters. Try to ensure that meetings have a strategic dimension to them, such as reviewing current activities, thinking about future opportunities and trends. This can help ensure whether the current plan is still on the right track and identify when any changes need to be made.

Check that the assumptions behind the plan are still valid

In any planning process assumptions about the future are made (such as 'the number of volunteers will remain the same' or 'referrals will stay at the same rate'). It is useful to record the main assumptions you make so that you can review them in the life of the plan. If the assumption proves to be incorrect the plan might need rethinking.

What to consider when updating the plan

It is much better to change a plan deliberately and clearly than to let things drift or ignore the plan. The following issues should be thought through when you update or change the plan.

- **Consider the size of the change.** Is it a temporary blip or a minor issue which doesn't fundamentally change the direction of the plan? Is the change so significant that it makes the existing plan's premise outdated or no longer credible? A major issue will clearly require a rewrite of the plan while a more minor issue might just involve the reordering or reprogramming of the operational plan.

- **Take something out for everything that goes in.** If you change the plan this usually involves more work. A useful rule is that for every new task, commitment or piece of work the organisation will have to move resources from somewhere else and therefore reduce resources and time spent on an existing commitment in order to do something new.

- **Communicate the change.** It is important to communicate changes in a plan to relevant parties. Staff need to understand how the new plan might affect their work. It is also worthwhile to talk with key funders to ensure that they understand the nature of the change. This may involve having to renegotiate expectations.

It is helpful to see the business plan as an ongoing and continual process rather than just a document.

Ten ways to use the plan

To steer the organisation

The plan should be like a road map for trustees and managers to help them stay on track to achieve the organisation's goals. They need to consult it regularly.

To monitor progress

At different points you should be able to show which parts of the strategy have been completed, which are in progress and which are struggling.

To explain your ideas and intentions to external parties

The plan should show the thinking behind the organisation's direction. Reading the plan should spell out the idea, the model and the assumptions that underpin it.

To evaluate new proposals

Ideas for new projects or spending should be tested to ensure that they fit with the direction set out in the plan.

To help people see the bigger picture

The plan should help people to see how their role fits into a bigger plan.

To persuade funders and commissioners to back you

The plan can provide funders with sound evidence that you have thought through your ideas, that they are realistic and that you have the capacity and expertise to deliver them.

To allocate resources

Budgets and work plans should take into account the plan's priorities. If it's not in the plan, then why are you doing it?

To identify success

When you achieve elements of the plan they should be acknowledged and celebrated.

To develop collaboration with potential partners

If you share your plans with similar organisations you can start to identify areas for joint working and collaboration or, at the very least, to avoid duplication.

To meet procurement tests

Commissioners often require a business plan as part of the procurement process so that they can check that the organisation is sound, well-managed and has a coherent plan.

References

Brookes, Martin (2002), *Funding our Future: Understand and Allocate Costs*, London, Association of Chief Executives of Voluntary Organisations

Charity Commission (2010), *Charities and Risk Management*, www.charitycommission.gov.uk/media/94007/cc26text.pdf, Crown Copyright

HM Treasury (2002), *The Role of the Voluntary and Community Sector in Service Delivery: A Cross Cutting Review*, London, Crown Copyright

Lake, Neville (2012), *The Strategic Planning Workbook*, London, Kogan Page

Mintzberg, Henry (1978), 'Patterns in Strategy Formation', *Management Science*, vol. 24, no. 9, pp. 934–948

McKinsey & Company (1980), 'The 7-S framework', www.mckinsey.com/insights/strategy/enduring_ideas_the_7-s_framework

Osterwalder, Alexander and Yves Pigneur, *Business Model Generation*, Hoboken NJ, John Wiley and Sons

Index

What else can DSC do for you?

Let us help you to be the best you possibly can be. DSC equips individuals and organisations with expert skills and information to help them provide better services and outcomes for their beneficiaries. With the latest techniques, best practice and funding resources all brought to you by our team of experts, you will not only boost your income but also exceed your expectations.

Publications

With over 100 titles we produce fundraising directories and research reports, as well as accessible 'how to' guides and best practice handbooks, all to help you help others.

Training

The voluntary sector's best-selling training – 80 courses covering every type of voluntary sector training.

In-house Training

All DSC courses are available on your premises, delivered by expert trainers and facilitators. We also offer coaching, consultancy, mentoring and support.

Conferences and Fairs

DSC conferences are a fantastic way to network with voluntary sector professionals whilst taking part in intensive, practical training workshops.

Funding Websites

*DSC's funding websites provide access to thousands of trusts, grants, statutory funds and corporate donations. You won't get more funders, commentary and analysis anywhere else. Demo our sites **free** today.*

Trust**funding**.org.uk
Government**funding**.org.uk
Company**giving**.org.uk
Grantsfor**individuals**.org.uk

Visit our website today and see what we can do for you:

www.**dsc.org.uk**

@DSC_Charity
For top tips and special offers

Or contact us directly: publications@dsc.org.uk